The Transformation Principle

Do not be conformed to this world, but be transformed by the renewing of your mind, that you may prove what is that good and acceptable and perfect will of God.
Romans 12:2

The Transformation Principle

TABLE OF CONTENTS

SECTION   **PAGE**

Participants In The Transformation Program

LEADER: Enlists and trains encouragers and directs the Transformation group. Teaches leader time segment. Has been trained in a Transformation group for a minimum of two cycles and has completed all homework.

ENCOURAGER: Has completed one Transformation cycle. Has been approved by the unit leader.

ENCOURAGER APPRENTICE: Is enrolled in a Transformation group and has made a commitment to a 17-week cycle.

CLIENT The emotionally unstable or person enrolled in a Transformation group. Must make a 51-week commitment.

PRAYER PARTNER: Each encourager involved in the program will enlist a prayer partner outside the program. The prayer partner's responsibility is to pray _for_ both the encourager and the encouragee daily. The prayer partner is to pray _with_ both weekly.

The Transformation group consists of a 51-week program. This 51-week program consists of three 17-week cycles. All of the support material is covered in 17 weeks, and the cycle is repeated twice more for those in the program.

Cycle #1	_Information cycle_	17 weeks
Cycle #2	_Application cycle_	17 weeks
Cycle #3	_Maintenance cycle_	17 weeks
		51 weeks

The Encourager will stay with the assigned Client through the Information and the Application cycles (34 weeks). He/she is the Client's support person. During the maintenance cycle, the Client will relate directly to the leader.

Weekly group meetings will consist of:

30 minute Group Leader Time - A lecture by the leader on material that has been studied the previous week.

30 minute Encourager Time - One-on-one time for Client and Encourager to review material, make assignment for the upcoming week. This is the best time to deal with personal problems.

30 minute Positive Group Time - Here we share positive goals and victories.

The Transformation Principle

Week 1

Introduction

The Transformation groups began with a promise that was made by Jesus Christ. He promised "If the Son shall set you free, you shall be free indeed". (John 8:36). I had come face to face with the fact that, though a person had entered into a personal relationship with Christ, too often that same person was still being controlled by destructive habits and emotions. These were destroying the person's life.These root problems chained them to a very destructive lifestyle from which they could not break free.

The Transformation program is a journey to freedom. We gain that freedom as we allow Christ to show us how we can truly be free. After many hours of counseling others and through study of addictions and associated problems, I became aware of the basic root problem common in every case: Man is separated from God, and his wrong attitudes keep him from the only source of real help for his problems. Real freedom can only occur when deep-rooted destructive attitudes have been changed.

I. *Grasping the Basic Concept*

It is our estimation that at least 75% of our decisions are made by our subconscious mind, independent of our conscious minds. The subconscious makes these decisions based on the principles fed into this unique computer we call our mind. Once our subconscious decides on a course of action, it then forces us to carry out its decisions.

- How our subconscious overrides our conscious mind.

Emotions are used to insure that we respond to our mind's suggestions. We all know that emotions can be much stronger than reason. This leads us to the conclusion that, since the majority of our decisions are made by our subconscious mind, we will be able to effect a significant change in our life only if we can change the decisions made there. **The Transformation Program is a tool designed to help us do this.**

II.   *The Root Problem*

The problem is that our subconscious operates off the false principles of the world and the negative information we are fed day by day. As we deal with all the guilt, fears, and frustrations of day-to- day life, our mind becomes saturated with those things. We are offered the world's answers to our problems, and our minds learn to operate by those principles. Due to the fact that these principles are faulty and often lead to greater problems, we sink deeper and deeper into despair and hopelessness. We become enslaved in a destructive lifestyle and can find no way to break free. As we dwell on our failures and addictions, the bondage increases. As we struggle to tear ourselves from this quicksand, we are just carried further and further down.

III.   *Changing From the Inside Out*

If we are to be successful in changing, we must change at the subconscious level -- the level which the Bible refers to as the "heart". After we have spent a lifetime of saturating our mind with harmful thoughts and attitudes, there is only one thing that is powerful enough to change us. Our only source of real help is God's Word -- **the Bible.** There are reasons that the Bible is such a powerful tool:

A.   THE WORD CLEANSES – (John 15:3 "You are already clean because of the word which I have spoken to you."

Jesus told His disciples that they were cleansed through the washing of the Word. The truth of the Bible neutralizes the lies and false promises by which we have learned to live. Jesus tells us that knowing the truth is essential to freedom. (John 8:32). God's Word is the ultimate source of all truth.

B.   THE WORD HAS LIFE WITHIN ITSELF

As we saturate our minds with God's Word, the Holy Spirit takes that powerful weapon and uses it to transform our lives from within.

IV.   *Our Goal*

The **Transformation Program** is designed to fill the participant's mind with God's Word and thus effect the desired change. We do this three ways:

1. Regular Bible Study to nourish the mind. (Luke 4:4)

2. By training the subconscious to use the basic principles taught in God's Word.

3. Saturating the mind with verses that teach a truth that will combat a specific problem in the participant's life.

STUDY SHEET - WEEK 1

Memory Verse: For the word of God is living and powerful, and sharper than any two-edged sword, piercing even to the division of soul and spirit, and of joints and marrow, and is a discerner of the thoughts and intents of the heart. Hebrews 4:12

DAYS 1-6   Each day review the material for week 1 in the manual.
Spend time with God in prayer then record a blessing received for the day.

Day 1   Reflection question: Give an example of a task you can perform without thinking about the specifics related to accomplishing that task.
Additional study passage - 2 Corinthians 10:3-6

Day 2   Reflection question: Explain why a person who lives by God's principles will always be successful in the good life.
Additional study passage - Psalms 15:1-5

Day 3   Reflection Question: What is the one area in your life you would most like to change? Are you willing to do the work necessary to accomplish that change?
Additional study passage - Colossians 3:14-17

Day 4   Reflection Question: Why would positive healthy change be impossible without Christ's help?
Additional study passage - John 5:39

Day 5   Reflection Question: Why is real and permanent change in our lives not likely to happen immediately and will happen in time only if we are willing to do the work change requires?
Additional study passage - Mark 4:26-32

Day 6   Reflection Question: Why is it most important to saturate our mind with the positive promises from God's word rather than the negative passages?
Additional study passage – Philippians 4:8

OBJECTIVE 1

TO BE ON A SURE FOUNDATION

WEEK TWO *The Foundation*

WEEK THREE *Looking Inward*

WEEK FOUR *God's Faithfulness*

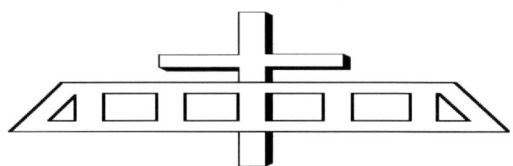

The first priority when rebuilding our lives is to lay a good foundation. God instructs us (I Corinthians 3:11) that the only secure foundation is Jesus Christ. He is the rock.

We were created for fellowship with the Supreme God. The only way that sinful man can fellowship with Holy God is through the God-man, Jesus Christ. As I identify with Christ and learn to live by and trust His promises, every area of my life is permeated by His power.

Week 2

The Foundation

The one who heeds Jesus words "is like a man building a house, who dug deep and laid the foundation on a rock. And when the flood arose, the stream beat vehemently against that house, and could not shake it, for it was founded on the rock" (Luke 6:48). The Bible states, "For no other foundation can anyone lay than that which is laid, which is Jesus Christ"   (I Corinthians 3:11).

It is impossible for us to rebuild our lives until we first lay a sure foundation. Just as the key to building a solid house begins with a sound foundation, so it is when we are attempting to build a solid life. The key to success in any rebuilding program is this: ***We must be on a sure foundation.*** The only foundation for a sound life is to be spiritually joined to Jesus Christ.

GOD DESIRES A RELATIONSHIP WITH US

God created us for fellowship with Him. What I want most from my children is their love and respect. I am thrilled to just be a part of their lives. God values us for the same reason. As I draw close to Christ, I sense His pleasure in our relationship. My heart answers with joy.

FIRST - GOD'S OFFER TO US

God's offer to each of us is stated in the Bible (John 3:16), "For God so loved the world that He gave His only begotten Son, that whoever believes in Him should not perish but have everlasting life". Here we find God's gift is eternal   - *life without end* (Romans 6:23). We don't work for it and we can't buy it, because gifts are not earned nor are they purchased. Rather, gifts are for receiving. Once received, the giver (God) grants ownership to us, and once we receive it, we have this life without end.

Since God's gift is eternal, He is preparing a permanent home in heaven with Christ for us. Jesus said, "And if I go and prepare a place for you , I will come again and receive you to myself, that where I am there you may be also." (John 14:3). He is the King of Kings and Lord of Lords of all creation, so wherever He is has to be the very best place.

This new life, however, does not begin when we die. It actually begins when we open our lives to Jesus Christ. Jesus said, "I have come that they may have life, and that they have it more abundantly." Abundant life is something God has made possible for us through His Son. So often we feel that the advantage of salvation begins in Heaven. However, God has prepared a wonderful life for us here. This abundant life is ours as we walk daily with him.

SECOND - THE ONE HINDRANCE TO MY RELATIONSHIP WITH GOD

Once I realized that God loved me and wanted me to always be with Him, I also became aware of the fact that my sinful nature kept me from Him. God is good, just and holy and cannot fellowship with sin. Regardless of how much God desired a relationship with me, I knew it could not happen as long as sin remained in my life.

The first man and woman enjoyed a daily walk with God that was only interrupted by their own rebellion. The sin that separated Adam and Eve from God was disobedience to God's command not to eat fruit from a particular tree. I know we have all done worse than that. Today man lies, steals, uses God's name in vain, etc. Because the payment for sin is death (Romans 6:23"), to pay the sin debt for one lie or even one selfish act would require eternal spiritual death (separation from God). Man is surely in a mess without God's help.

THIRD - HOW GOD SOLVED THE SIN PROBLEM

God's answer to the sin problem is Jesus. Jesus said, "I am the Way ... No one comes to the Father except through me." (John 14:6). Jesus is the only one who can bring us to God.

Jesus is God and became man. (See John 1:1&14). Jesus existed in the beginning. The Bible teaches us that everything that was made was made by Him. He was and is a spiritual being. However, it was only when a virgin (Mary) conceived of the Holy Spirit of God that Jesus became man. He put on an earthly house (the Bible's reference to the physical body). So Jesus, who already was God, became man and lived among men. He is the God-Man.

Jesus died on the cross for our sins. God's Word says, "For Christ also suffered once for sin, the just for the unjust, that he might bring us to God (I Peter 3:18)." Because our sins separate us from God and the penalty for sin is death, Jesus willingly died our death for us. Because Christ has paid our sin debt, Holy God can now have fellowship with sinful man. Christ's death is the only provision for forgiveness for sin that God has made. There is salvation in no other. He died that we might live.

Yes, Jesus is the answer to the problem of our separation from God because of sin. However, He can have no effect on our lives unless we receive Him. (Now please read John 1:12). We can see that it is necessary that we receive Jesus.

FOURTH - THE CHOICE IS MINE

The choice as to whether I spend eternity with God or I am eternally separated from Him is mine. No one can make that decision for me; this one is between me and God. If I choose Christ, I must be willing to turn from my sin and turn to Him. Before I met Christ, I was going away from Him. The day I invited Him into my life I turned from my sin to Him. In the Bible this is referred to as "repentance". I must also be willing to give him control of my life. He certainly knows better than I what is best for my life. My trust must be in Him and Him alone for eternal life.

FIFTH - HOW I RECEIVE HIM

When I received my wife in marriage, the Bible teaches that we became one flesh. Jamae became a blood relation to me and, because of her relationship to me; she became a blood relation to my father. Just as my wife's relationship to my father was made possible by the commitment she made to me, in the same sense my spiritual union with Christ made possible my relationship with God the Father. Have you invited Christ into your life? If not, why not do so now?

PRAYER OF COMMITMENT

"God, I know that I have sinned. Please forgive me. I know that Christ died for my sin.

I also know He arose from death and wants to be a part of my life. I invite Him into my life and receive Your gift of eternal life. My desire is to live for You and serve You.

I know You are preparing me a place in heaven with You and I will be with You there. Thank You for that wonderful hope. Amen."

STUDY SHEET - WEEK 2

Memory Verse: Jeremiah 29:11 "For I know the thoughts that I think towards you, says the Lord, thoughts of peace and not evil, to give you a future and a hope."

DAYS 1-6   Each day review the material for week 2 in the manual.
Spend time with God in prayer then record a blessing received for the day.

Day 1   For Reflection: State the mental picture you have of a life that has a sure foundation.
Additional study passage: I Corinthians 3:11-15

Day 2   Reflection question: What do you think heaven will be like?
Additional study passage: Revelation 21:1-5

Day 3   Reflection Question: How do you deal with feelings of guilt in your life?
Additional study passage: - II Corinthians 7:9-10

Day 4   Reflection Question: If God asked you, "Why should I let you into heaven?", what would you say to Him?
Additional study passage: - 1 Peter 3:15-16

Day 5   Reflection Question: What do you think is meant when we are instructed to "receive Jesus"?
Additional study passage - John 1:1-13

Day 6   Reflection Question: How do you give Christ control of your life? Is He in control of your life now?
Additional study passage - Ephesians 5:8-14

Week 3

Looking Inward

It seems that there is a conspiracy out there to bring us to the place where we focus our attention strictly on our needs and ourselves. We all seem to be trying to find out who we are and are constantly being encouraged to get to know ourselves. Some religious groups try to put us in touch with our inner-selves: we are directed to discover the person within us. Therapists focus their patient inward in order to discover what went wrong. But is all this looking inward healthy, or is it actually creating more problems? We will seek to answer this question in this lesson.

THE PROBLEM WITH LOOKING INWARD

When we look inward, it is impossible to be objective. When focusing our attention on ourselves, one of two things occur: we focus our attention either on (1) the positive, seeing ourselves as wonderful, or (2) the negative, concluding that we are terrible. It is impossible to be objective when examining our innermost self. Our emotions get in the way. We either magnify the positive and become filled with pride, or exaggerate the negative and decide we are worthless. We examine ourselves and think we are either the greatest person who has ever lived or the worst; we are either god or the devil. We feel that everything exists to benefit us or we think everything and everybody is against us.

In my work I find that when a person is trying to explain to me what they are really like, they magnify either their good qualities and minimize the bad, or they magnify the bad and minimize the good. They see themselves as either very good or very bad. I rarely feel that I am getting a clear picture of what they are really like. I must discover that for myself as I get to know them.

Since we are unable to be objective, it is easier for an emotionally stable person close to us to know us than it is for us (by looking inward) to get a balanced and clear picture of who we really are. After a few months of working with a person, I am very sure that I have a better idea of what he is like than he himself does.

THE POSITIVE FOCUS	*THE NEGATIVE FOCUS*
--Magnify the positive--	--Magnify the negative
I can do no wrong	*I can do nothing right*
The world owes me	*I don't deserve anything good*
I never have to say I'm sorry	*It's all my fault*
My actions were not that bad	*I made a fool of myself*

What we are looking for here is honesty-- which is, in reality, truth. We want to relate to God, others and ourselves in a positive way, but only after we have dealt with the negative in our lives. The worst thing we can do is to ignore the negatives that keep us from being the person God intends for us to be. The secret is to let Truth (Christ) show us who we really are. When we turn our attention on Christ we see ourselves as Christ sees us. We see an example of this in Isaiah 6, when the prophet saw the Lord high and lifted up he confessed, "I have unclean lips". He had been saying things that were not nice. Peter upon meeting Christ exclaimed. "Depart, oh Lord, I am a wicked man". Both these men went on to fulfill their part in God's great plan. They achieved greatness through their relationships with the Lord.

THE END RESULT OF THE INWARD LOOK IS INSANITY

When we look inward, we see an angel or a devil; the wisest man on earth or the dumbest, the good person or the bad. Since we never get a clear picture of who we are, we become confused and disoriented. The more we turn inward, the more confused we become which causes us to turn inward even more. Soon we become so confused that we give up trying to find out who we are and imagine in our mind the person we would most like to be and then pretend to be that person. This pretend life only causes one to become more unreal or plastic. I have known people who would choose someone they admired and live their life as if they were that person, trying to act like or do the things they think that person would do. At other times we may invent a person and try to become that person rather than the person we really are. We can readily see why this would lead to insanity and frustrate the will of God for our lives. If you fall into this trap you will never become that special person God created you to become.

If we focus our lives outside ourselves and on Christ we become real. Early in my ministry I had been aware that something was worrying my wife. When I asked her what was wrong she refused to talk about it. One day she came to me and said she had to talk to me. She told me that for some time she had been unsure of her salvation. She felt it was terrible for a pastor's wife not to be sure she was saved. I had no doubt as to my wife's salvation, but I wanted her to be very sure. I asked her where she was looking for assurance of salvation. Her answer was that she was looking within her heart. I told her that she would never find assurance of salvation there, that her assurance was in Christ Jesus. I was rewarded with a smile. That was the last of her problems in that area. Now when she needs assurance, she just looks to Jesus.

Below is a simple test I use in my counseling. I have found that generally the higher the score, the healthier the mind. You test yourself, but be very honest; you only hurt yourself if you rate yourself either too high or too low. We are looking for an accurate picture here.

THE INWARD/OUTWARD TEST

A	B	C	D	F

I.   GOD

I attend church, pray, study His Word and seek Him to worship and honor Him

To have my needs met

II.   OTHERS

I develop relationships to meet their needs

To have my needs met

III.   INTERESTS

I develop interests and hobbies to minister to others

To have my needs met

SCORE

I._____

II._____

III._____

Average score _____

The closer to "F", the more serious the problem

CHRIST IS THE STANDARD--STUDY HIS LIFE--RETAKE THE TEST

STUDY SHEET - WEEK 3

Memory Verse   Matthew 6:33 "But seek first the kingdom of God and His righteousness, and all these things shall be added to you.

DAYS 1-6   Each day review the material for Week 3 in the manual.
Spend time with God in prayer then record a blessing received for the day.

Day 1   Reflection Question: List some reasons why it is unwise to focus inward. What serious problems does looking inward promote?
Additional study passage - Philippians 2:12-16

Day 2   Reflection Question: What are some social problems prevalent in our society today that would fade if the people of our nation were focused more outward and less on themselves?
Additional study passage - James 3:13-18

Day 3   Reflection Question: Why would looking inward cause me to feel that I must justify or excuse my actions to others or perhaps even myself?
Additional study passage - Philippians 3:12-15

Day 4   Reflection Question: Why would focusing on getting the things that I desire hinder me getting them or, once received, stop me from being able to enjoy them?
Additional study passage - Mark 4:14-20

Day 5   Reflection Question: Why do you think that it would be difficult to find out much about yourself by looking inward?
Additional study passage - Psalms 25:12-15

Day 6   Reflection Question: Our relationship with God does not improve by focusing inward it only gets more complicated. Why would this be so?
Additional study passage - Psalms 63:1-5

Week 4

God's Faithfulness

I often have people come into my office in the inner city asking for money to avert some disaster in their lives. I explain that we will not give them money, but will try to find them the help they need--if they can substantiate that they are "on the level." The usual response is, "You don't trust me?" To which I reply, "I don't know you. Without knowing you, how could I trust you?"

Trust has to be based on knowledge of the person and their character and actions in the past. Until I know you or until your reliability is verified by someone I know and trust, I have no reason to either trust or distrust you. If we are wise, we learn to base trust on past performance.

When we look to God, His faithfulness is beyond question. He has proven Himself faithful in every instance, and we have the Bible as a record of His trustworthiness. We can see how He has kept His word throughout the history of the world. We have a record of hundreds of promises He has made which still apply to us today. In every instance He has kept His word. If we are ever to have a meaningful life, we must learn to trust God. The terms "faith" and "trust" are interchangeable. His Word says that without faith (trust), it is impossible to please Him.

Since knowledge of a person is important in developing trust, it is evident that the better we know our Father in heaven, the more we will trust Him. *To know Him is to trust Him*. Once we truly know Him and the fullness of His love, we will trust him.

Let's look at some ways by which we get to know Him better.

1)   *Spend time with Him.*

2)   *Note the promises He has made to His children* and His faithfulness in keeping those promises.

3)   *Study the lives of men who have demonstrated an intimate walk with God* and the evidence of God's faithfulness in their lives.

1) *Spend time with Him.*

God created us for fellowship with Him. He wants us to know Him. Certainly we cannot know God apart from Jesus Christ. In John 14:6, Philip asked Jesus to show them (the disciples) the Father and they would be satisfied. Jesus' answer was, "If you had known me, you would have known my Father also." The only approach to God is through Jesus. Now the way to know Christ--and in turn, the Father--is through spending time with Him. We do this through reading His Word, the Bible, and spending time in prayer.

2) *Study His Promises.*

The quickest way to determine a person's reliability is to look at the promises he has made in the past and at his track record in keeping those promises. Is he a person of his word? Now God not only has an excellent record (there are thousands of references to His faithfulness), but He also invites us to test Him for ourselves. (Malachi 3:10).

3) *Study the lives of men who have walked with God.*

Throughout history, God has used men to accomplish His purpose here on earth. The lives of these "men of God" are very often documented in great detail, both in the Bible and through biographies. As a new Christian, I studied the lives of these men and discovered a common thread in their lives. As they learned to trust God and to rely on Him completely, God was always more than faithful. This was a tremendous faith builder in my own life.

OUR ASSURANCE

Once we have established the fact that God can always be trusted, we need only to look at the promises related to our salvation to know that we are secure in Christ Jesus. I am referring to promises like John 3:16, where God offers us everlasting life if we receive Jesus, or Romans 6:23 where it states "... the gift of God is eternal life through Jesus Christ," or Romans 10:13 that tells us whoever calls on the Name of the Lord shall be saved. Also read John 10:27-30, I Corinthians 3:11-15, Romans 8:31-37, and John 3:17-21, 36. I want to close this session with one verse. We need to memorize and hold it close to our hearts. "In hope of eternal life which God, who **cannot lie, promised before time began." Titus 1:2**

STUDY SHEET - WEEK 4

Memory Verse: "In hope of eternal life which God, who cannot lie, promised before time began." Titus 1:2

DAYS 1-6:   Each day review the material for Week 4 in the manual.
Spend time with God in prayer then record a blessing received for the day.

Day 1   For Reflection: Recount the time you can first remember the Holy Spirit drawing you to the Lord.
Additional study passage - John 6:44, 12:32

Day 2   Reflection Question: In your dealings with your fellow men, what have you based trust on in the past?
Additional study passage - Psalm 118:8-9

Day 3   Reflection Question: Is there any promise you have discovered in God's Word that has special meaning for you?
Additional study passage - Jeremiah 17:7-8

Day 4   For Reflection: Consider some tactics Satan might use to keep us from trusting God's promises.
Additional study passage - II Timothy 2:22-26

Day 5   For Reflection: Give thought to possible bad consequences in our lives if we lose faith in God's eternal salvation.
Additional study passage - Galatians 3:1-7

Day 6   For Reflection: Consider possible eternal benefits for ourselves and for others in sharing our confidence and trust in Christ.
Additional study passage - I Thessalonians 5:8-11

OBJECTIVE 2

TO BE OF A SOUND MIND

WEEK FIVE   *Emotions and a Sound Mind*

WEEK SIX   *Building Our Bridge of Faith*

WEEK SEVEN   *Renewing the Mind*

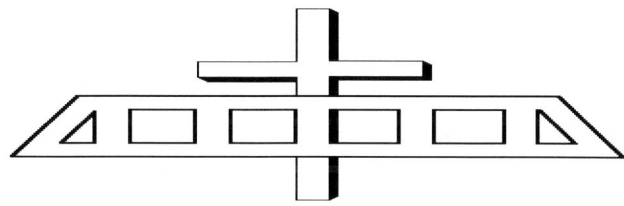

Realizing that we can only have a healthy fulfilled life if we have a healthy mind and that uncontrolled emotions are the greatest deterrent to a healthy mind, our goal is to bring our thoughts and emotions into conformity to the principles and purpose of God. We need to grasp the fact that our best decisions are made at that place of emotional stability and that we can control our emotions, rather than have our emotions control us.

Week Five

Emotions and a Sound Mind

We live in an emotionally unstable generation. Much of what is classified as mental illness is, in reality, emotional illness. There may be many contributing factors, but the real problem is that we are trying to deal with emotions God never intended us to deal with.

When God created man, He didn't design man to deal with guilt. That is why He sent Jesus to take our guilt. God never intended for us to carry anger. That is why He warns us not to let the sun go down on our wrath. We are not designed to live in a state of fear or anxiety. We should trust God to take care of us.

These and other emotions destroy our emotional balance. They plunge us into depression and despair. This causes our body to try to bring us back to stability by releasing adrenaline and other chemicals in our body. However, because the basic problems are not dealt with, these chemicals cause these destructive emotions to intensify and we are driven lower and lower.

The world's method for dealing with these depressions is to use stimulants such as alcohol, drugs, music. or illicit sex to rise out of this pit of despair. Before long our emotional swings are like a roller coaster. We spend all our time either depressed or on an induced high. We have now become emotionally unstable.

If we are to be emotionally stable, these wrong emotions must be dealt with. We cannot allow them to control our lives. God's Word contains the only truly successful plan for this. We must saturate our minds with these great truths, but first let us look further into what it means to be emotionally unstable.

Characteristics of Emotional Instability:

1. We don't follow our reason but are controlled by our emotions. We may know what is best, but find ourselves giving in to our emotions and doing what is unwise.
2. We spend most of our time depressed or bored. We are constantly seeking a high or a thrill. We live for a high time.
3. We make the major decisions for our life when we are emotionally high or low. (This is the only time we really have the courage, false though it may be, to make these decisions.) Our decisions are based more on how we feel than on sound reason.

Emotional instability destroys a sound mind. Here is a diagram that helps us see the relationship of our emotional level to having a sound mind.

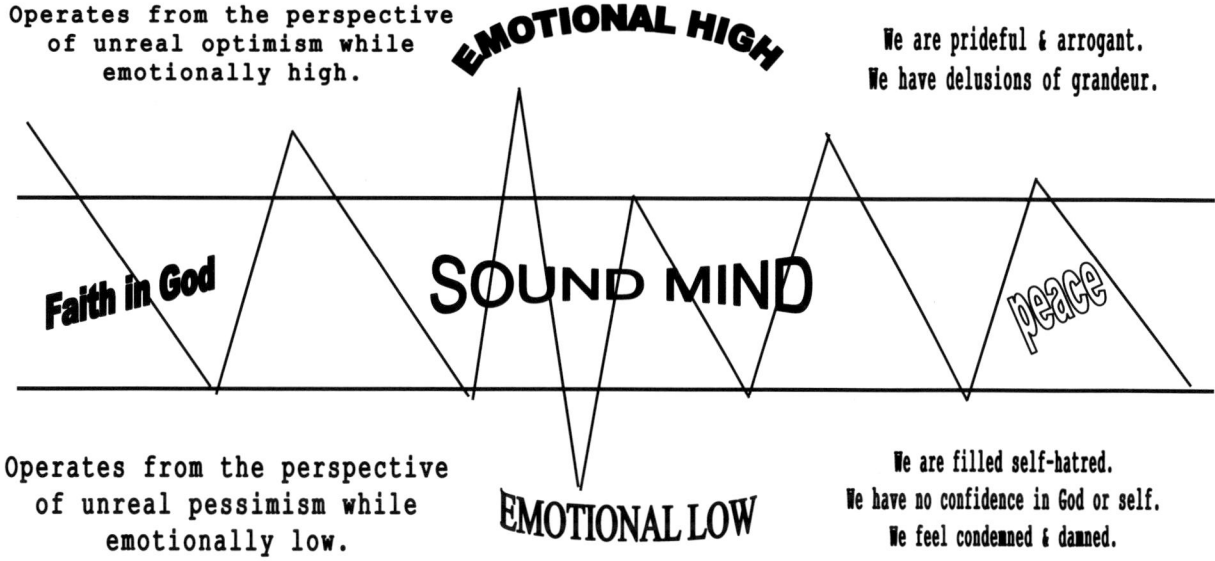

Operates from the perspective of unreal optimism while emotionally high.

EMOTIONAL HIGH

We are prideful & arrogant.
We have delusions of grandeur.

Faith in God

SOUND MIND

peace

Operates from the perspective of unreal pessimism while emotionally low.

EMOTIONAL LOW

We are filled self-hatred.
We have no confidence in God or self.
We feel condemned & damned.

When we are carried by our emotions, we spend most of our lives in the upper or lower regions of our emotional curve. We cannot deal with life effectively at either the high or the low points. The higher we go, the more optimistic we become. We are puffed up with pride. We are the center of the universe - everything revolves around us.

At the other extreme, we sink into depression. There is no answer to our problems. Our life is without purpose, and no one really cares. Why should they? We are worthless and useless. It is at this point we often desire to end it all.

We only make the best decisions when we are emotionally stable. *That stability should become our goal.*

Benefits of Emotional Stability:

1. **It is the quality God is looking for in His leaders.** In fact, it is a quality any person must have to be a good leader. Notice the qualities God demands in His leaders. These are found in I Timothy 3:1-13. It is obvious that what is pictured here is a person who is stable.

2. **It allows us to do our most realistic and logical reasoning while making decisions.** This is one reason why Christ encouraged His disciples to find that place of peace that only He offers (John 14:27). It is why the writer of Hebrews urges us

to enter into that place of rest (Hebrews 4:9-10). The prophet Elijah heard the still, small voice of God only when he had calmed down. Elisha called for music to soothe him before directing the armies of Israel and Judah in the wilderness during a time of great distress.

3. **One of the greatest benefits of emotional steadiness is that we can control our emotions.** Too many times people let their emotions control them. God loves giving us wisdom (a sound mind), but He cannot, even if we ask, unless we are emotionally stable. Read carefully James 1:5-8. There is no promise here for wisdom from God unless we are emotionally stable.

Steps to Stability:

1. **Desire peace and a sound mind rather than desiring thrills, highs, and worldly pleasures.** (God has promised us the desires of our heart -Psalm 37:4). This must be a conscious decision.

2. **Determine never to make major decisions while emotionally high or low.** Learn to recognize "red flags". These are actions, things, places, etc. that let you know you are in dangerous territory.

3. **Seek God as soon as depression or emotional elevations occur.** Stay with God until He brings you back to emotional stability.

PRIDE - LIFE IN THE FAST LANE

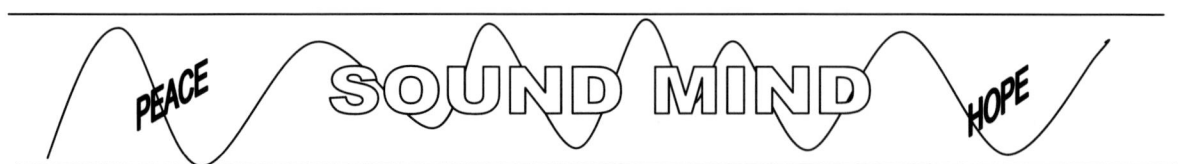

SELF DEBASEMENT

Once our life is stable, we can become an anchor for others who need us.

Daily Emotions Tracking Graph

Sunday	Monday	Tuesday	Wednesday	Thursday	Friday	Saturday

10

9

8

7 — — — — — Above this line we are prideful — — — — —

6

SAFE ZONE

5

4

3 — — — — — Below this line is a sense of hope lessness — — — — —

2

1

0

STUDY SHEET - WEEK 5

Memory Verse: "For to be carnally minded is death, but to be spiritually minded is life and peace." Romans 8:6

DAYS 1-6 Each day review the material for Week 5 in the manual.
Spend time with God in prayer then record a blessing received for the day.

Day 1 Reflection Question: Do you normally make decisions when you are emotionally stressed or when you are at peace?
Additional study passage Isaiah 32:15-19

Day 2 Reflection Question: Can you remember a time when, under emotional stress, you made a wise decision? Can you remember an unwise decision made because of stress?
Additional study passage - Isaiah 57:19-21

Day 3 Reflection Question: Why would it be a mistake to make important decisions when we are emotionally high?
Additional study passage - Hebrews 4:1-2

Day 4 Reflection Question: What are some attitudes and trends in our society today that create an unstable environment?
Additional study passage - Mark 6:30-32

Day 5 Reflection Question: Considering the nature of God, why would stable emotions be an asset in having a close relationship with the Lord?
Additional study passage - Psalm 120:6-7

Day 6 For Reflection: Share your thoughts on why a stable life would be a benefit in improving all our relationships.
Additional study passage - Philippians 4:4-7

Week 6

Building our Bridge of Faith

God's Word teaches us that man is born to trouble. Life is never smooth sailing - it is full of depressions.

Often, when trouble comes, we face it with depression and despair or panic. Let us keep in mind that, when we are depressed and out of our emotional safety zone, we can no longer trust ourselves to make the wisest decisions. It is also important to understand that during these times of trouble, we need to make the wisest choices. We can only be assured of making the best choice when we have emotionally returned to the safety zone. However, it often becomes the pattern that we make our most important life decisions when we are in the pit of despair. Satan gives us a shovel, and we dig our hole deeper.

It is obvious that we can't escape the troubles. Even if we could somehow create a trouble-free life, it would not be best for us (James 1:2-4). It is important that we learn to cope with problems. It is through dealing with problems that we mature and grow emotionally and spiritually. God understands that dealing with problems is important in shaping a healthy life, but He never intended that we deal with these difficulties alone.

This leads us to two important questions. ***First,*** *how do we keep from sinking into despair when faced with problems? And* ***second,*** *once we sink, how do we get out and avoid digging our hole deeper?*

FIRST-How to Stay Out of the Abyss of Despair?

The answer is that we build a bridge of faith. A strong faith in God and His promises will keep us steady during the worst storms. A strong bridge of faith that will support us during the difficult times does not just happen. It must be carefully constructed using the materials God has given us. Now, let's learn how our faith bridge must be constructed.

The two main supports for our bridge are:

1. God's Word (specifically, God's Promises)
2. *Prayer* (claiming those Promises) James 4:2 states "You have not because you ask not."

We support our bridge through regular prayer and Bible study

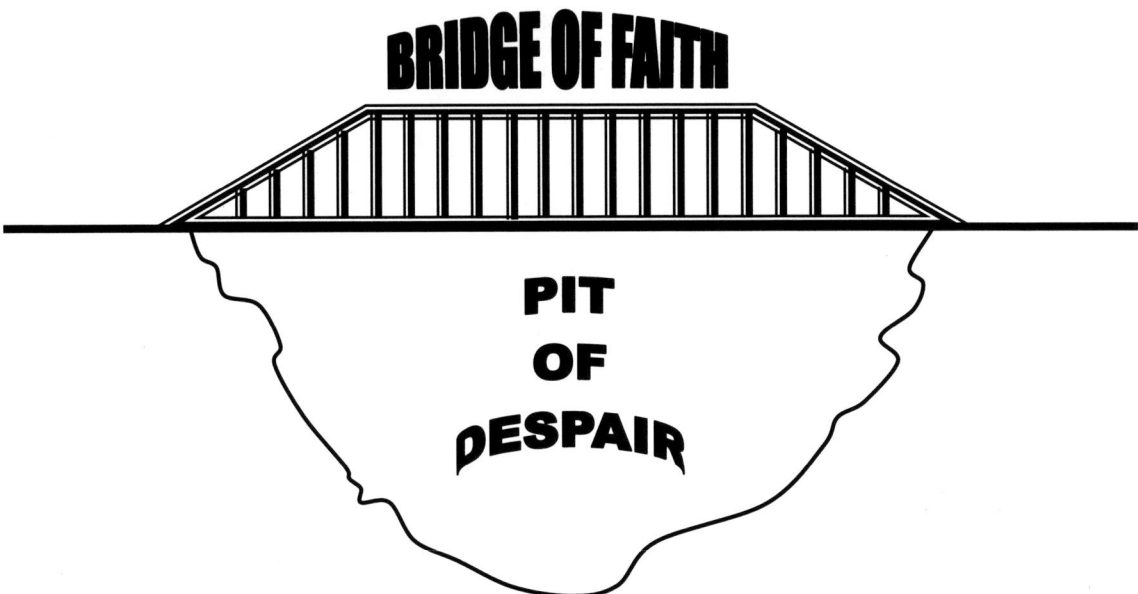

Once we have our supports in place, we can begin to work on the specifics of our faith. We will refer to these as the "planks" of faith. These planks correspond to the attributes of God and the areas of our lives that require faith in God to see us safely over a troubled time. To have a secure bridge, these planks must be strong. We begin strengthening our bridge by working on the weakest planks first.

Let's look at all the attributes of God listed below and think about which might be the "weak planks" in your life: (This would be a good time to look in your "Bridge of Faith" booklet and **read the descriptions of these attributes.**)

God's **Love:** *John 3:16*
God's **Forgiveness:** *Acts 10:43*
God's **Salvation:** *John 1:12*
God's **Provision:** *Isaiah 41:13*
God's **Total Awareness:** *Proverbs 15:3*
God's **Protection:** *II Samuel 22:31*
God's **Presence:** *Psalms 46:7;11*
God's **Goodness:** *II Chronicles 5:13*
God's **Unlimited Power:** *Ephesians 1:19-20*
God's **Deliverance:** *Psalms 56:3-4*
God's **Guidance:** *Exodus 15:13*
God's **Timing:** *Ecclesiastes 3:1, 11a*

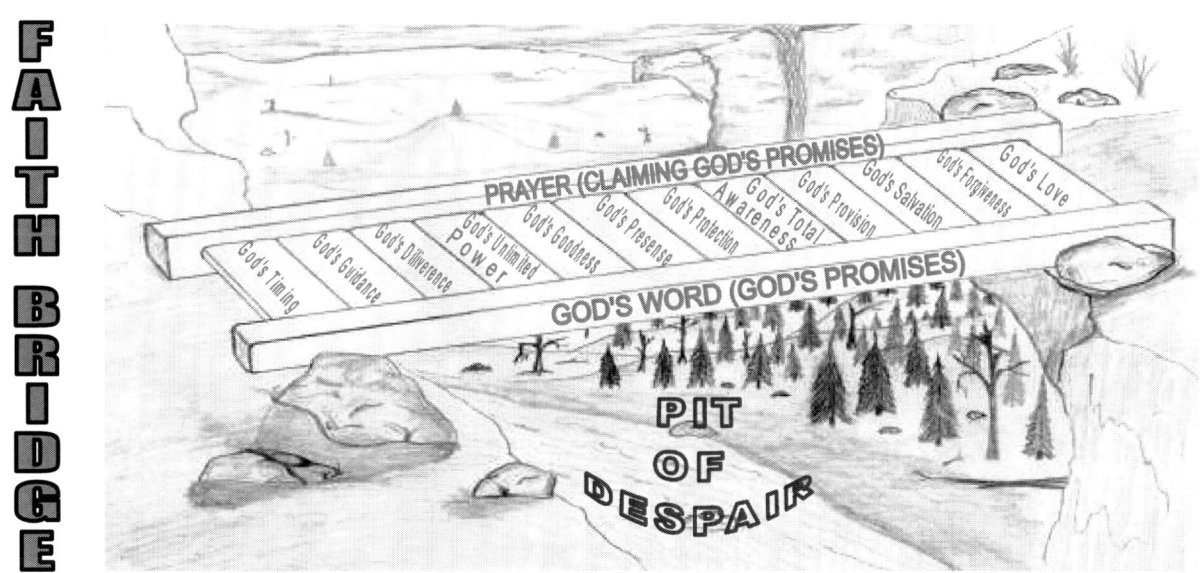

Once he has built a strong faith, it is possible for an emotionally unstable person to become stronger and more stable than a person who has never been an addict or had noticeable emotional problems.

SECOND-*How do we get out once we find ourselves in the pit?*

Peter showed us the avenue of escape when he found himself sinking during his walk of faith, having taken his eyes off Jesus to look at the storm. He knew his only hope was Jesus. "Jesus, help!" was his cry.

Christ is attentive to our cries for help. I am convinced that this Transformation program is Christ's answer to those who have found themselves hopelessly lost in the storms of emotional bondage or addictions. I believe that Christ has given us the steps that, coupled with your faith, will result in your deliverance.

Christ has the answer to all life's problems. No problem will ever exist that He doesn't have the answer for. **HE IS GOD.**

STUDY SHEET - WEEK 6

Memory Verse: "You will keep him in perfect peace, whose mind is stayed on You, because he trusts in You." Isaiah 26:3

DAYS 1-6: Each day review the material for Week 6 in the manual.
Spend time with God in prayer then record a blessing received for the day.

Day 1 Reflection Question: What two disciplines are essential in order to keep our Bridge of Faith from collapsing? Why?
Additional study passage - II Chronicles 14:11-12

Day 2 Reflection Question: When considering the twelve planks in your Bridge of Faith, which do you believe to be your strongest and which your weakest?
Additional study passage - Romans 15:13

Day 3 Reflection Question: Once we have located a weak plank in our Bridge of Faith, how do we strengthen it and make it "quake-proof"?
Additional study passage – Habbakuk 2:4

Day 4 Reflection Question: Why is it important, when we are in a faith-building program, that we choose our companions--and even conversations we take part in--with care?
Additional study passage - I Corinthians 15:33-34

Day 5 For Reflection: What are some accepted attitudes in our society that work to undermine our faith in God.
Additional study passage - I Corinthians 2:3-5

Day 6 For Reflection: Find the weakest plank in your Bridge of Faith (page 2, Week 6) and devise a plan to make it your strongest.
Additional study passage - Romans 10:16-17

Week 7

Renewing The Mind

Romans 12:2

The Communists discovered that a man could be told a lie long enough and often enough and he will accept that lie as the truth. They call this "brain washing". The world used this approach to sell its so-called New Morality. This philosophy says to do what feels good to you. If you want a live-in lover, or to drink, or do drugs, or get an abortion, that is OK. It is your body; you can do what you want. We have reached a point in our nation that we can't tell right from wrong.

God also knew that it is important that He repeat the same truths often in order for us to grasp or even accept the truth as truth. He commanded that His word be taught over and over again, beginning when a person was young. As we study God's Word and saturate our mind with God's Principles, we are truly "brain washing". Jesus talked about the washing of the Word. What the Communists and the world are doing is not brain-washing; it is really "brain polluting"! If we are to have true success, we must saturate our mind with truth. John 8:32 says, "You shall know the truth and the truth shall set you free."

The great need is for us to renew our minds. Read carefully II Corinthians 10:3-5. So often we feel that we have little control over our thoughts. That is simply not so, although that is exactly what Satan wants us to think.

In order to understand how we can renew our minds, we need to be aware of the way our mind functions. We are told that only 13% of our mind is conscious, while 87% is unconscious or subconscious. Information passes through our conscious mind and is stored in the subconscious. We are told that everything that has ever passed through our conscious mind is stored there. However, it is not always easy for us to bring it back out once it has been stored. It is also true that whatever is in our subconscious mind greatly affects our life. What we have stored in our subconscious mind is constantly spilling over into the conscious. Our subconscious mind will most often give back what is closest to the surface and those things with which it is saturated.

That is why, when we go to the store, we must keep repeating our shopping list. Otherwise, we forget. Even though our mind records all, it is not long before what we have taken in is buried in our subconscious mind, and only a hypnotist can recover the information. We remember best what has happened most recently and those things we think about most often. If our thoughts are bad or unhealthy, our subconscious becomes saturated with garbage. This garbage affects everything we do. If our subconscious mind is filled with fear, doubt, and distress, our whole life becomes filled with these things. Jesus tells us that what is in our hearts affects all that we say or do. (I am convinced the heart here refers to the unconscious mind). Please read Matthew 12:33-37.

Once our mind has become saturated with unhealthy thoughts we form self-destructive patterns of dealing with the emotions that arise from these thoughts. These cycles we refer to as SSD (subconscious self -destruct) cycles. Once these cycles are firmly in place in our subconscious mind, they are very difficult to break. We all develop different ways of dealing with these emotions. At the end of this lesson I have given two examples of these destructive cycles. You should be able to develop your own work sheet plotting the SSD cycles in your life. Keep in mind that when breaking these, you have to break them at the earliest possible point. Once you allow the cycle to get started, your emotions will force you to follow through to the end.

THE WAY OUT

There are two things we must be concerned with here:

> *(1) How do we cleanse our minds?*
> *(2) How do we break the destructive patterns already set?*

I.   *HOW WE CLEANSE OUR MINDS*

It has already been mentioned that it is possible for things to become buried in our mind. Our memory is clearer on what happened yesterday than what happened last year. Time is the great eraser. For instance, we remember very little of what happened in our early childhood.

Knowing that we can bury memories simply by refusing to think about or dwell on them makes our task easier. Some memories need to be buried and left behind. (These memories and thoughts need to be scripturally dealt with before they are buried. This will be explained fully in later studies during the Transformation program). We want the surface of our mind filled with only the best. This is what God's word teaches us in Philippians 4:8. There He has given us a list of those things He would have us saturate our minds with. If we are to be successful in changing our life, we must change the things we think about.

In order to renew our mind, there are two things we must do.

A. *We must deal with destructive thoughts and memories.* We want these buried deep within our mind so they will lose their power to affect our conscious mind. We must train our minds to refuse unhealthy thoughts.

B. We must fill our mind with those things suggested in God's word. We must replace unwanted thoughts with God's word and principles. The Transformation program of study has been designed to help with this.

II. BREAKING DESTRUCTIVE PATTERNS

A. *We must break old cycles at the earliest possible point.* The easiest time to short circuit an old pattern of behavior is before they become charged with emotion. Most often we cannot control the things that trigger a SSD cycle, but we can control the way we react. We must learn to immediately refocus our attention on the Lord. He is the source of true peace and a sound mind. Once we are in control of our emotions, we can then apply the principles that apply to problem solving (week 9).

B. *We do this by developing a whole new lifestyle.* We develop new interests, new friends, new priorities, new goals and new attitudes. We will work to create healthy habits and patterns of living. Once we form these new patterns, they will become as hard to break out of as the old ones are now. We also must learn to live in the emotional safe zone, where our mind works best.

C. *Use the chart provided to plot destructive patterns in your life.* The two examples provided are from actual clients (used by permission). You may need more than one sheet. As you proceed through the transformation process allow the Holy Spirit to reveal these unhealthy cycles to you and guide you as you break and replace them with healthy cycles. Your leader can help with this.

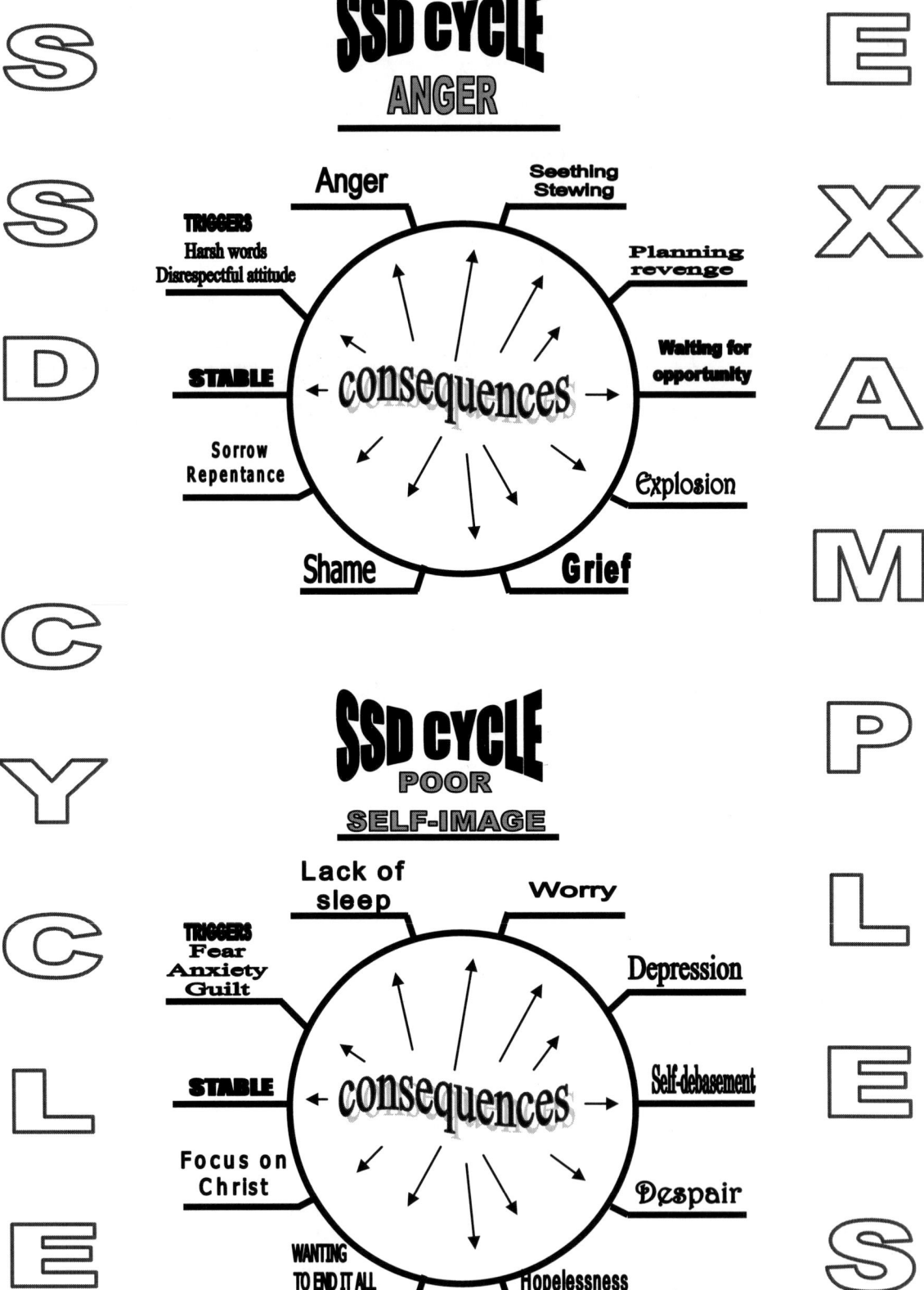

SSD CYCLE
ANGER

Anger   Seething Stewing

TRIGGERS
Harsh words
Disrespectful attitude

Planning revenge

STABLE   consequences   Waiting for opportunity

Sorrow Repentance

Explosion

Shame   Grief

SSD CYCLE
POOR SELF-IMAGE

Lack of sleep   Worry

TRIGGERS
Fear
Anxiety
Guilt

Depression

STABLE   consequences   Self-debasement

Focus on Christ

Despair

WANTING TO END IT ALL   Hopelessness

S S D C Y C L E   E X A M P L E S

33

SSD CYCLE

_____

TRIGGERS

STABLE

consequences

STUDY SHEET WEEK 7

Memory Verse: Do not be conformed to this world, but be transformed by the renewing of your mind, that you may prove what is that good and acceptable and perfect will of God.

Romans 12:2

DAYS 1-6:   Each day review the material for Week 7 in the manual.
Spend time with God in prayer then record a blessing received for the day.

Day 1   Reflection Question: When you consider your mental diet, is what you are putting into your mind going to have a good or a bad effect on your life?
Additional study passage - II Corinthians 10:3-6

Day 2   Reflection Question: When we consider the conversations in which we participate, the TV we watch, the books we read, etc., estimate the percentage of the information you receive daily that is positive. What percentage is negative?
Additional study passage - Matthew 15:17-20

Day 3   Reflection Question: What are some positive steps you can take to improve your mental health?
Additional study passage - Philippians 4:6-8

Day 4   Reflection Question: When you lay in bed at night, do you often review the slights and wrongs that you have experienced?
Additional study passage - Hebrews 4:9-12

Day 5   Reflection Question: What is your earliest childhood memory? Is it pleasant or unpleasant?
Additional study passage – Ezekiel 11:19-21

Day 6   Reflection Question: Would you say that you control your thoughts or that your thoughts control you?
Additional study passage – Psalms 119:28-31

OBJECTIVE 3

TO BE RESPONSIBLE

WEEK EIGHT   *Fixing Blame*

WEEK NINE   *Problem Solving*

WEEK TEN   *What is Smart and What is Not*

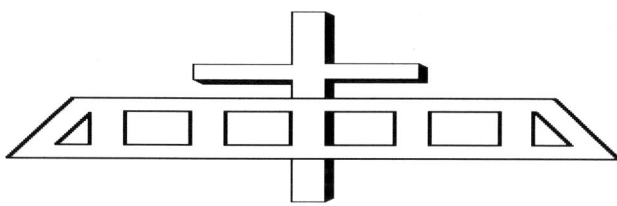

Because being responsible means accepting responsibility for my decisions and actions, and because my being responsible is vital if I am to be a mature person, I purpose to learn to be accountable in every area of my life. Christ is the greatest example of what it means to be responsible. We will learn from His Word the secret of success.

Week Eight

Fixing Blame

It is a rare person who is honestly satisfied with his or her life. Few feel that they are accomplishing anything worthwhile and, because our lives are not what we want them to be, the obvious question is: *Who is responsible for the mess I find myself in?* Our first tendency is to look around for someone else to blame. Our friends often support us in this desire to fix the blame elsewhere. However, their opinions lack the authority and weight of someone with training and the proper credentials. Some psychiatrists and professional counselors make a lot of money helping us find someone else to blame for our sorry lives. Fathers, mothers, brothers, sisters, employers, friends, society and God are all very handy when we need a villain.

The fact is, though, shifting responsibility --while it may make us temporarily feel better-- does not solve our problems, nor does it change our lives. All we have done is paint someone else "wrong" so that we will appear " right". **The only way we will improve our situation is to firmly accept responsibility for our own lives.** Is it better to convince ourselves that we are not responsible for a misdeed, or to take responsibility and allow God to completely cleanse us and bring His healing into that area of our life? The obvious answer is that it is better to be cleansed and healed. We benefit greatly when we do not turn to alibis but honestly accept full responsibility for our actions. This, however, is not simple, because the emotion of pride gets in the way.

I am convinced that it is pointless to seek excuses for failure. The potential for success or failure is within people themselves, regardless of circumstances. A willingness to take complete responsibility for our own actions, coupled with faith in God, assures us of real success. **Success has less to do with our situation than how we face that situation.** The Bible is full of those who faced difficult situations only to rise to greatness.

Joseph was a slave who became Pharaoh's right hand, a mighty ruler of Egypt. The king placed **Daniel**, a slave, over the kingdom of Babylonia. **David**, a shepherd, became a king. It seems that God delights most in using those whose success shocks and confounds the world. Look at those He chose as His disciples.

If we are to be successful in life, there are three attitudes, which are musts.

     1)   We will accept full responsibility for our actions and the results of our decisions.

     2)   We will focus on past failures only to learn from them. We will learn to give them to God and use them only as stepping-stones to success.

     3)   We will see difficulties and abuses as opportunities for growth as we are strengthened through faith in Christ.

1)   We must accept full responsibility for our actions and the results of our decisions.

We are always eager to accept credit when we have made good and wise choices. If we are to be honest, we must also accept blame when we have made unwise decisions. It is a fact that when we refuse to accept blame for unwise choices, we continue to repeat those same unwise decisions. By refusing to accept responsibility, we are dooming ourselves to repeated failure. Others lose confidence in us and are disgusted by our unwillingness to be responsible. Although we may convince ourselves that we are not to blame, rarely is anyone else fooled.

It is also true that ***we must accept responsibility for our wrong actions to be forgiven***. Jesus made the statement, "The well do not need a physician." As long as we are proclaiming our innocence, we will never see a need to ask Christ to forgive and cleanse us. Confession (admitting to sin) is the first step to forgiveness. Read I John 1:9. When the prophet Nathan confronted King David with his sin, David humbly stated, "I have sinned," and Nathan immediately responded that God had forgiven him. Once we admit our sin and turn to Christ, He stands ready to forgive. *Is it better to acknowledge o*ur sin and receive God's forgiveness or excuse and retain our guilt?

2)   We will focus on past failures only to learn from them.

As you remember from our lesson "Renewing the Mind," one of the keys to having a sound mind is what we place into our subconscious mind. If we constantly dwell on our past failures, we program ourselves for failure. We need to think on good and wholesome things. Thoughts such as "I am glad I went through that because I learned this valuable lesson" are good. However, when we repeatedly go over past failures, we become saturated with failure, and we begin looking for someone else to blame.

Once we have received God's forgiveness and learned what there is to be learned, we must forgive ourselves and forget. Sometimes, we ask God's forgiveness but continue to condemn ourselves. If we are going to continue to condemn ourselves after we have asked God for forgiveness, then Christ died in vain as far as we are concerned. God tells us that when He forgives sin, He forgets it and remembers it no more. Why do we remind Him by dwelling on our forgiven sin? We must learn to forgive ourselves and quit dragging our sin back up as a dog drags up rotten meat. Besides, only Christ can forgive Sin. You can't forgive yourself. You can only accept His forgiveness and cleansing.

3)   *We will begin to see difficulties as opportunities.*

      The people we most admire are those who have overcome huge difficulties on their climb to greatness. We tell these stories over and over again. Our war heroes became heroes during difficult, sometimes impossible, situations. We love those who beat the odds and triumph over disaster.

      The heroes of the faith are men and women who, by faith, faced trouble and difficulties as conquerors. Hardships are opportunities for us to test our faith. The Bible says to count it all joy when you fall into trouble. (James 1:2).

STUDY SHEET - WEEK 8

Memory Verse: Do not be deceived, God is not mocked; for whatever a man sows, that he will also reap. For he who sows to his flesh will of the flesh reap corruption, but he who sows to the Spirit will of the Spirit reap everlasting life.

Galatians 6:7-8

DAYS 1-6: Each day review the material for Week 8 in the manual.
Spend time with God in prayer then record a blessing received for the day.

Day 1 Reflection question: When you are faced with guilt for something you have done, what is your normal way of dealing with that guilt?
Additional study passage - Ezekiel 18:30-32

Day 2 For Reflection: After we have made commitment to God are we held accountable by God if we decide keeping that commitment is not convenient or to our advantage and then back out?
Additional study passage - Deuteronomy 23:21-23

Day 3 For Reflection: Tell how, by acting responsibly, we can turn our mistakes into benefits in our lives and in the lives of others.
Additional study passage - Luke 8:38-39

Day 4 For Reflection: Consider why shifting blame to others does not relieve you of the responsibility for your own actions. Give your reasons as to why this is so.
Additional study passage - Genesis 3:9-13

Day 5 Reflection question: What is the one decision God charges us to make that will determine whether we will spend eternity in heaven or hell? Have you made that decision?
Additional study passages - John 1:11-13

Day 6 For Reflection: When we refuse to accept responsibility for our actions, we forfeit many blessings God has promised His children. Name as many of these lost benefits as you can think of.
Additional study passage - Psalms 1:1-3

Week 9
Problem Solving

Spiritual maturity is evidenced by our confidence/courage in facing difficult situations, our problem solving abilities and our ability to establish healthy relationships. In this lesson we will focus on problem solving. We will attempt to defuse emotions that rob us of the ability to do our most realistic and productive problem solving. Our world is crying for someone who can face problems with a clear and cool head.

I.   *CLEARING THE DECK*

It is impossible for us to be a good problem solver if we are trying to deal with too many problems at one time. While in the Marines, I was trained to be a electronics technician. In order to locate the problem in a defective piece of equipment, we often had to work on it live. There were often thousands of volts of electricity inches from our fingertips. It did not take many stiff shocks before we learned to keep our attention on the problem at hand. In the same way, if we are distracted from a problem that needs our attention, we are likely to get burned. Our first priority must be clearing our mind of all but the problem at hand.

A. We must get rid of the anticipated or imagined problems. God will not assist us with problems that do not presently exist. God is realistic and practical. He will not become involved in or encourage our delusions when we try to solve problems that do not yet exist.

It is not the real problems that cause the most concern in people's lives. It is those pesky anticipated problems. It seems that for every here-and-now problem, there are ten potential problems waiting in the wings to steal away our peace of mind. The most often repeated scene in my office are those similar to the one I will share here.

A man I work with had gone to the doctor in great pain. The doctors had wanted to do the surgery immediately after the problem was diagnosed. There was no doubt that surgery was needed. The operation to fix the problem was relatively simple, and not to have the surgery was life-threatening. On this day his state of anxiety was at the highest level that I had seen in months. "I have decided that I am not going to have the surgery," he told me. When I inquired why on earth not, he told me that he had been given a list of possible complications. "I can not possibly deal with these," he informed me. He had gone through his list of complications one by one and determined that he was incapable of dealing with all of this. I quickly pointed out that he had one real problem and twenty anticipated problems, and that he was suffering all the emotional trauma that he would experience if he actually had twenty-one medical problems. (Our emotions cannot distinguish between the real and the expected). He was suffering emotional overload. We decided that he was capable of facing his one real problem, especially since the scheduled surgery would solve that problem. It was unlikely that he would have even one of those twenty complications. The surgery would solve the problem at hand and, if he did experience a complication, he would still only have one problem. He left my office in good spirits - he could deal with one problem. (The surgery was successful with no complications).

Since an anticipated problem causes all the emotional trauma experienced when a problem truly exists, piling on expected problems is a quick way to a nervous breakdown. The emotional trauma related to all our worries renders us mentally incapable of effectively dealing with the legitimate problems that we face daily in our lives.

B. We are to release those problems that we have no control over. God does not expect us to solve all the world's problems-- only He could do that. (He has shown you, O man, what is good; and what does the LORD require of you but to do justly, to love mercy, and to walk humbly with your God? Micah 6:8) As I make my first priority my walk with Christ, He directs me to that need where I can make a difference. He will often use me to be part of the solution to a problem; but when I try to fix every thing in sight, I could hinder God in His purpose of working something good in the lives of those involved in that situation. God does use problems to bring us to him and build spiritual maturity in our lives.

The key to knowing which problems to involve ourselves in is having a healthy walk with Christ. Not only will we experience the inner peace He brings, but He also eliminates the confusion and wasted effort that is often so much a part of our lives.

C. We must put aside those problems that are better dealt with later. When solving problems, God's timing is primary. God will only assist us today with those problems that are to be dealt with today. If we want God's help with our problems we must accept His timing. (1) Knowing when to move on a problem is only made possible by a heart soft toward God. It is impossible to determine something as sensitive as God's timing if there is any rebellion or unconfessed sin in our lives. (2) Often, when we ask God what we should do, His answer is "Wait." (3) However, we must have the faith/courage to go when God says to go.

II.   *STABILIZE EMOTIONALLY*

A. Focus on Christ -Jesus is the answer to all our problems, but He is also the source of any real peace in our lives. His unequaled wisdom, His ability to bring peace in the midst of any storm, His more than adequate power for any situation makes Him the logical first choice when we are in need. His promise that He will never leave us is priceless when we are in distress. ***God has infinite answers for any real problem I face (He has only one best answer).***

B. Practice scripture saturation -The best tool for calming the spirit is <u>God's</u> <u>Word</u>. It still amazes me how soon that one well-chosen verse can calm troubled and bruised emotions. While reading passages like the 23rd Psalm is great when we are in distress, I feel in using scripture saturation we not only are calming our emotions, but have the added benefit of conditioning our subconscious mind against future anxiety.

C. Pray -James tells us that we have not because we ask not. It is tragic that we so often ignore our one source of real help during times of trouble. While problem solving we should be constantly aware of Christ's loving presence. The Holy Spirit is especially attentive when our problems overwhelm us. He makes our needs clear to God even when we can't.
(<u>Remember</u> <u>the</u> <u>principles</u> <u>you</u> <u>learned</u> <u>in</u> <u>week</u> <u>5</u> <u>on</u> <u>emotions</u> <u>and</u> <u>a</u> <u>sound</u> <u>mind</u>)

Problem solving formula: **SIFT**
>   <u>S</u>**ingle out real problems**
>   <u>I</u>**solate the problems that are the most urgent**
>   <u>F</u>**ind God's absolute best solution**
>   <u>T</u>**ake action as soon as a wise decision is reached**

STUDY SHEET - WEEK 9

Memory Verse: "Therefore do not worry about tomorrow, for tomorrow will worry about its own things. Sufficient for the day is its own trouble. Matt 6:34

DAYS 1-6: Each day review the material for Week 9 in the manual.
Spend time with God in prayer then record a blessing received for the day.

Day 1 *Reflection question*: When you are faced with a problem, what is your normal way of dealing with that problem?

Additional study passage – Psalms 138:7-8

Day 2 *Reflection question*: What is your emotional state while dealing with a difficult situation? What should it be?
Additional study passages - Psalms142:1-7

Day 3 *For Reflection*: Consider three reasons why God would be unwilling to become involved in our anticipated or imagined problems.
Additional study passage - Philippians 4:6-7

Day 4 *For Reflection*: Tell how, by acting responsibly, we can turn our problems into benefits in our lives and in the lives of others.
Additional study passage- 2 Corinthians 4:16-18

Day 5 *For Reflection*: Explain how we harm those who are close to us when we do not deal responsibly with our problems.
Additional study passage - Jonah 1:7-12

Day 6 *For Reflection*: Describe a situation where you felt you dealt with a difficult situation in an appropriate manner. Was there a sense of satisfaction at being a successful problem solver?
Additional study passage- Joshua 1:9

Week 10

What Is Smart and What is Not

Real success is determined by our ability to make wise choices. We often see a person rise to greatness out of a difficult situation simply by making wise choices. There is little hope or help for someone who persists in making bad choices.

In order to make wise decisions, wisdom is required. We will, for our study here, define wisdom as "the ability to determine the best course of action and to take that course." It does very little good to know what is best if we refuse to act upon that wisdom. Therefore, we are to set our hearts on wisdom, and we must desire to gain the knowledge required to determine what is best -- then follow that course.

There is a trap that we sometimes fall into: although we don't want to make bad choices, we are often willing to do those things that come close to, but fall just short of, what we consider wrong. We use phrases such as, "Just show me in the Bible where it's wrong to take a social drink, or smoke pot, etc."

People often seek me out as a minister to share some questionable practice in which they are involved. They often try to pressure me into agreeing that what they are doing is all right, as if my saying that their actions are acceptable will assure them that they are fine. The very fact they seek my approval is evidence that they have doubts about those actions. If I disagree, they then consider me an enemy and usually they continue the same course of action anyway.

I have learned not to always pull out the Bible in the first instant, but to simply ask the question, "Is this the best way?" Is it better to drink or not to drink? Is it better to take drugs or not to take drugs? For a reasonable-minded person the answer is simple. That opens the door for me to explain that God wants the very best for us, and we should refrain from asking what we can get away with. Instead, we need to ask ourselves what is truly best. Since so much is riding on our choices, we had better give attention to making the right decisions.

We have already stated that wisdom is related to two facts: Knowing and Doing. Let me share a few suggestions related to these two areas.

First, Knowing: The Bible says, "You will know the truth and the truth will set you free."

1. *We can prepare to make wise choices by studying the wisdom books and passages in the Bible.* I know some very wise men who make it a point to read a Proverb a day. They read the chapter which corresponds to the day of the month. This should be done in addition to other reading in God's word. We need the whole counsel of God.

2. *Use mature Christian counselors.* Those people who have demonstrated victory in their own lives can be invaluable when we need honest advice. The Bible informs us that God has given us pastors, teachers, and exhorters to help us make wise choices.

3. Always ask the question, "Is this really the best?" We need to ask that question in the light of God's Word and His purpose for our lives as we understand it.

Second, Doing: **Sometimes knowing is easy; doing is the hard part.** Most of us are controlled by our feelings and thus make disastrous choices. Here are some suggestions:

1. *Stay away from places and people who increase temptation or have an unhealthy influence on us.* Read the first chapter of Psalms. Notice what God asks us to do if we want to be blessed.

2. *Learn to hang onto God during the difficult times.* Temptations pass if we will spiritually reach out to God during the rough times. Look to Jesus and just hang on.

3. *Make no provision for accomplishing that which is not best.* We should do our best to push out of our mind any thought that is not the best. If we allow ourselves to think about it -- even though we determine not to do it -- then we are only one step away from falling prey to a bad decision. If we don't allow ourselves to think about it, we are two steps away. We need that extra margin of safety. If we dwell on the thought in a moment of weakness, we will fail. Don't let Satan entice you to think about those things that are not best.

STUDY SHEET - WEEK 10

Memory Verse: "Therefore if the Son makes you free, you shall be free indeed." John 8:36

DAYS 1-6: Each day review the material for Week 10 in the manual. Spend time with God in prayer then record a blessing received for the day.

Day 1 For Reflection: Explain why God gave man a will.
Additional study passage - I Kings 18:21

Day 2 Reflection question: Which has the strongest hold on individuals today - reason (logic) or emotions? What emotions most often cause you to make unwise choices?
Additional study passage - Deuteronomy 30:15-16

Day 3 Reflection question: What do you consider the driving emotion that led to Satan's disastrous choices in heaven?
Additional study passage - Isaiah 14:12-14

Day 4 Reflections question: How do you relate man's freedom of choice to man's freedom in Christ Jesus?
Additional study passage - John 15:13-14

Day 5 Reflection question: Why is it natural for us to seek others to condone our actions when we know in our heart that we didn't make the best choice?
Additional study passage – 1 Samuel 15:18-22

Day 6 Reflection question: Since your whole life is shaped by the choices you make, what do you feel is the most significant thing you can do to assure you make the best choices?
Additional study passage - Joshua 1:7-8

OBJECTIVE 4

TO BE ABLE TO RESOLVE CONFLICTS

WEEK ELEVEN   *Relationship Inventory*

WEEK TWELVE   *Short Cut to Destruction*

WEEK THIRTEEN   *Processing Your Anger*

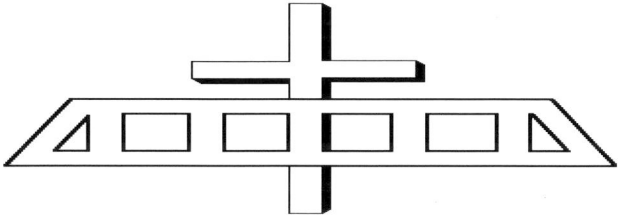

Building good relationships is possibly the point of greatest difficulty. Unhealthy relationships destroy us; healthy relationships make both parties better. The key to having healthy relationships is having a healthy relationship with Christ. How we relate to Him has a profound effect on all other relationships. Here we will discover some revealing truths that will guide us as we seek to build and restore relationships.

Week 11

Relationship Inventory

Mark 12:31 states, "And the second commandment, like it, is this: You shall love your neighbor as yourself." We are social beings and are so from birth. I am told that in a large hospital, it was discovered that the babies closest to the nursery door were healthier and happier. Those in the back of the room fared much worse. We understand the reason for this. Even though all the babies' physical needs were met, the ones out front were getting most of the attention. The solution was to rotate the babies.

In prison, isolation is considered one of the harshest forms of punishment. We have realized in America that loneliness is one of our most severe social problems. There is no way we can measure the avalanche of other problems faced by our society that stem from loneliness.

The fact is, we need others. God has created in us the basic human need to be cared for and loved. We go to great lengths and considerable expense attempting to gain love and acceptance. The con-man takes advantage of this tendency. The advertiser often cashes in on this need in order to help sell his goods or services. "We care about you," he promises.

We try to satisfy this social need through physical bonds. Our tendency is to seek to attract relationships through the five senses.

1. In order to look our best, we diet, prim, exercise, tan, make-up and make-over. All is done to make ourselves more pleasing to the eyes. We want the world to see us looking good. Our society supports a host of designers, stylists, cosmetic surgeons, make-over artists, and dental specialists trying to keep us looking our best.

2. We also want to sound good. We work on diction and phonics. We rehearse in our minds what we are going to say. When we hear someone who sounds good to us, we try to imitate them. We want to learn the dialect as soon as possible when we move to a new part of the country, so we will fit in. We hear ourselves on tape and determine never to open our mouths again. "I didn't know I sounded that bad," we say.

3. How we smell is also important. We shower, spray, powder and deodorize all in an attempt to smell good. Our favorite perfume may cost $100 or more an ounce. Boys must smell one way and girls another. And horror of horrors if we get the smells reversed.

4. We also use the sense of taste as means of social interaction. The good cook says, "I hate cooking just for myself." We often hear observations such as, "The way to a man's heart is through his stomach." We are all aware of the social value of food.

5. Finally, we need to touch. How often have I heard someone say, "I just wish I had someone to hug." We hug, hold hands, and kiss. Many people seek a church that will provide them with the hugs they need. Kids climb into parents' laps seeking that special hug, and young people practice hugging that special person for hours on end.

Yes, we use all our senses in an effort to gain the social acceptance that is a basic need in all our lives; and although we seek to establish these relationships using our five senses, no interaction just through our physical senses is completely satisfying. The relationship that fulfills deepest needs must be on a spiritual level. No other will satisfy. We were made for fellowship with a spiritual God. This spiritual relationship we so desperately need is called **bonding.**

The most serious problems related to caring for babies who are born addicted to drugs (because of drug-addicted mothers) is that these babies will not bond with their mothers or with anyone. For most babies, bonding is a natural process that occurs with the mother before the child is born. I have to ask myself the question, "Do addiction problems hinder our ability to bond with others?" If they do, what's God's answer to this most serious problem?

One observation I have made is that **true bonding is not on an emotional level--it is on a spiritual level.** Since bonding takes place on a spiritual level, the hindrances to that interaction must also occur on a spiritual level. If we are having problems relating to others, there must be a definite spiritual reason.

Shielding

"Shielding" is a term we use to describe the process of spiritually shutting others out. The common phrase used is "putting up walls". The use of "walls" implies **permanence, when, in reality, we are able to lower our shields to admit those whom we consider to be no threat to hurt us, or to cause us unpleasantness.**

Before we are ready to attack the problem, we need to find out how well we relate to those who are closest to us and, if there are problems that hinder those relationships, what they are.

1. We need to make a list of people who are closest to us. Start with those we have known longest--father, mother, siblings, husband, children, employer, co-worker, etc.

2. We should also list any problems that exist in that relationship.

3. We need to list any undesirable emotions we feel related to that person --anger, bitterness, jealousy, animosity, etc.

4. Last, we need to assess where we are justified in our feelings.

RELATIONSHIP INVENTORY WORKSHEET

Please list those you have established relationships with in order of priority, beginning with Number 1.

Relationship No. _____

A. **I have had a personal relationship with** _____
   for _____ years.

B. **I would classify my relationship with this person as:**

   1 - Very Good   2 - Good   3 - Fair   4 - Poor   5 - Love/Hate

C. **The emotions I most generally feel when I think of this person are:**
   (Circle all that apply)
   1 - Happiness   2 - Warmth   3 - Respect   4 - Love   5 - Confidence

   6 - Fear   7 - Hurt   8 - Anger   9 - Disappointment   10 - Bitterness

D. **If there are problems in your relationship with this person,**

1 -   ***Am I justified in my feelings toward this person?***
                       _____Yes   _____No

2 -   ***Why?***

STUDY SHEET WEEK 11

Memory Verse: "He who loves his brother abides in the light, and there is no cause for stumbling in him." I John 2:10

DAYS 1-6:   Each day review the material for Week 11 in the manual.
Spend time with God in prayer then record a blessing received for the day.

Day 1   Reflection Question: When making friends, name the three things you consider most important in this new relationship. What does Christ consider important?
Additional study passage - I Timothy 1:12-13

Day 2   Reflection Question: In reference to Question 1, do those things you consider important require "bonding" as defined in the study manual? If so, why?
Additional study passage – Psalms 15:3 & Proverbs 17:17

Day 3   Reflection Question: What are some wrong emotions that cause us to put up shields (walls) which hinder or make us unable to bond and form close relationships with God or others?
Additional study passage - James 4:4-8

Day 4   Reflection Question: What person do you most desire to form a strong bond (friendship) with? Do you have shields up in your life and, if, so, why are you reluctant to open yourself to that person?
Additional study passage - Proverbs 18:24

Day 5   Reflection Question: In your relationship with Christ, do you have shields up to protect yourself from Him? Explain.
Additional study passage - John 14:18-20

Day 6   Reflection Question: What spiritual victories are necessary in your life before close bonding (sharing) of your life with that of Christ's becomes a reality?
Additional study passage - I Peter 5:5-7

Week 12

Short Cut to Self-Destruction

The Bible states, "Do not be deceived, God is not mocked; for whatever a man sows, that he will also reap." Galatians 6:7.

I was startled to see the look of surprise on the young woman's face. I had just shared with her that bitterness is a sin and, as I observed her expression, I knew what was going through her mind. She was thinking, "How can this be a sin, when I was the one who was wronged? I have every right to be bitter." I could agree with her totally that she had been horribly and wickedly wronged, of this I had no doubt; but God would never allow me to agree that bitterness was good or acceptable. I knew that bitterness was slowly but surely destroying her.

The fact is, when we allow bitterness to take root in our lives, we suffer far more than the one we are bitter toward. That person may go on his way, never knowing or caring that we are bitter and, in some cases, would actually enjoy our misery if they knew. While the person we despise is often unaware of the fact, we are slowly but quite certainly destroying ourselves and everything good in our lives. Let's look at the disastrous consequences of bitterness in our lives.

1. *It will harm our physical health.*

2. *We become a slave to the person we are bitter toward.*

3. *Bitterness will affect every relationship in our lives.*

4. *It is a sin that will keep us from God's forgiveness.*

FIRST*,* **let's look at what bitterness does to our physical health.** Doctors tell us that close to 90% of all health problems are stress- related. Anger and bitterness are among the leading emotions that place stress on our physical bodies. Bitterness causes us to become tense.

Under this constant stress, our body has to work harder to accomplish normal functions. Over a period of time, we even show the effects of this stress in our faces. We begin to look "hard".

***SECOND,* we become slaves.** We are enslaved by our bitterness. We are emotionally tied to the person we are bitter toward. Everything they do or don't do affects us. We spend so much time nursing our animosity that we hinder our ability to have a useful and productive life.

***THIRD,* bitterness seeps over into every other relationship we have.** Read carefully Hebrews 12:15. Here it talks about a root of bitterness. A bitter spirit toward one person will spill over into every other relationship in our lives. It is like the rotten apple that spoils the whole barrel. It is a cancer that destroys us from within.

***LASTLY,* an unwillingness to forgive keeps us from having God's forgiveness.** Read carefully Jesus' instruction on prayer in Matthew 6:9-15. Especially note verses 14 and 15. An unforgiving spirit keeps you from God's forgiveness. It would also serve well here if you study Jesus' parable in Matthew 18:21-35. I am always touched by Jesus' comment upon first meeting Nathaniel, who became one of His disciples, "Behold, an Israelite indeed, in whom is no guile" (John 1:47). How easily those who are able to forgive and hold no grudges come to Jesus.

The Bible teaches us that knowing the truth will set us free. It is hard for us to practice good until we know what is good. Once we have recognized and accepted truth, we are free to practice truth. A person who does not know the truth is like someone blind in a strange place. That person stumbles around, never sure of himself.

For most of us, the first step to God has to be forgiveness toward those who have wronged us. We must not continue in unforgiveness, knowing that this is a path to self-destruction. In closing, I would leave you with this charge, "Forgive, and again I say, Forgive."

STUDY SHEET - WEEK 12

Memory Verse: "Looking diligently, lest anyone fall short of the grace of God; lest any root of bitterness springing up cause trouble, and by this many become defiled." Hebrews 12:15

DAYS 1-6: Each day review the material for Week 12 in the manual.
Spend time with God in prayer then record a blessing received for the day.

Day 1 Reflection Question: Do you have any health problems that you feel are stress-related and may be improved as you learn to properly deal with difficult relationships?
Additional study passage - Psalm 37:7-8

Day 2 For Reflection: Explain why bitterness and anger can be detrimental to our spiritual, as well as physical, health.
Additional study passage - Acts 8:18-23

Day 3 Reflection Question: Is there one person that -- were your relationship with that person improved -- your emotional health would improve? If so, who is that person?
Additional study passage - Proverbs 19:20

Day 4 For Reflection: Explain how learning to deal with relationships here on earth helps prepare us for heaven.
Additional study passage - Revelation 2:3-4

Day 5 For Reflection: Christ came to set us free. Consider why a person who has wrong emotions in a relationship cannot be really free.
Additional study passage - John 8:34-36

Day 6 Reflection Question: What one attitude is most important in our relationships with others? Describe this attitude.
Additional study passage - I Corinthians 13:1, 4-8

Week 13

Processing Your Anger

The Bible states, *"He who is slow to anger is better than the mighty, and he who rules his spirit than he who takes a city."* Proverbs 16:32

The young man had caught my eye a few days earlier. He was a physically strong, confidant, and polite boy of about sixteen whom I am sure the girls would consider a "hunk". Today, he had a cast on his hand, and his mother and his stepfather wanted me to talk with him. He had broken his hand when, in anger and frustration, he had jammed his fist into a wall. The anger and bitterness had been building up for some time, and he had held it all inside -- until the night before. Now he wore a cast on his hand. The anger, however, was still there.

Uncontrolled anger is a wicked emotion. Anger is never satisfied until we are completely enslaved by bitterness, which destroys every meaningful relationship and robs us of everything good and decent in our lives. The Bible tells us to be angry and not sin. Anger itself is not sin, but anger that is not dealt with and relinquished becomes bitterness.

Now that we have learned that uncontrolled or pent-up anger is not only bad for us personally, but it also displeases God, how do we deal with it? The world has two ways of dealing with anger. *The **first method** is through suppression or holding it in, and **the second** is venting -- letting it go or just doing what comes naturally when we get angry.*

Let us consider what is wrong with these two approaches.

FIRST, we have already seen what suppressed anger or bitterness does to our physical and mental health, to say nothing of our relationship with God. Because of the destructive nature of anger, we cannot afford to just keep it bottled up inside. Nothing is solved as long as we hold bitterness in; it simply continues to churn, waiting to erupt.

SECOND, we need to look at the practice of venting our anger. Seeing the deep and harmful effects of holding anger in, we have been taught that it is better to just let it out-- and this does give immediate relief. However, we feel better only temporarily. It doesn't solve anything.

Often we hurt others both psychologically and physically when we let loose, to say nothing of what we do to ourselves.

I was told of a man who was in the habit of holding his anger in. He was given a dummy on which to vent his anger and was encouraged to pretend the dummy was the person with whom he was angry. He was to take out his frustration by beating the dummy. This was fine for a while, until one day, in a fit of anger, he began beating his wife.

I hope you can see that both of these methods are equally bad. I am grateful that we are not left to the world's ways of struggling with anger.

The third method is relinquishing our anger. How do we do this without venting? We must release it to God. He is the only One who can effectively deal with it. Our Lord says, "Vengeance is mine." He desperately wants us to give our anger to Him. God warns us not to let the sun set on our anger. The key words for dealing with anger are "Forgive" and "Forget."

1. **Forgive.** Jesus had done nothing to harm the men who spat on His face, slapped Him, mocked Him, and nailed Him to the cross. Let's remember that these men also did not ask Christ to forgive them. However, Christ not only forgave them but asked the Father to forgive them as well. In the book of Acts, Stephen followed Jesus' example when he was being stoned to death. We need not wait for someone to ask our forgiveness before we forgive. One thing we must remember is that forgiving doesn't let *them* off the hook with God; it lets *us* off the hook with God. Once we have truly forgiven, the release that comes is the testimony that God is pleased.

2. **Forget.** How often have we heard the words, "I'll forgive, but I won't forget." The Bible tells us that when God forgives, He also forgets -- He remembers no more. Read Jeremiah 31:34. There is a very good reason why we must forget. When we remember a wrong that has been done us, our subconscious mind not only brings up the memory of the wrong done to us but also the emotions associated with the memory. Memories and emotions place us back where we started, and we have to deal with those things all over again. We spend our lives fighting the same useless battles over and over again.

STUDY SHEET - WEEK 13

Memory Verse: "Beloved, do not avenge yourselves, but rather give place to wrath; for it is written, Vengeance is Mine, I will repay, says the Lord." Romans 12:19

DAYS 1-6:   Each day review the material for Week 13 in the manual.
Spend time with God in prayer then record a blessing received for the day.

Day 1   For Reflection: List ways we try to punish those toward whom we are bitter.
Additional study passage - Ephesians 4:26-32

Day 2   Reflection Question: Why do you think so many couples state that their relationship improves after a fight? Does the making-up make the spat worthwhile?
Additional study passage - Colossians 2:6-10

Day 3   For Reflection: Explain how pride and anger are related.
Additional study passage - Proverbs 27:1-4

Day 4   For Reflection: Picture in your mind a man controlled by anger, one who is raging inside. While his anger burns, how wise will his choices be? How well will he be able to lead others? What are those around him feeling?
Additional study passage - Colossians 3:12-15

Day 5   For Reflection: Explain why uncontrolled anger makes us a slave and often an object of embarrassment and shame.
Additional study passage - Proverbs 21:7-9

Day 6   Reflection Question: Why does the Bible implore us to be slow to anger? Why are we often told to count to ten before we speak in anger?
Additional study passage - James 1:19-20

OBJECTIVE 5

TO BE CONFIDENT

WEEK FOURTEEN   *What is Truly Worthwhile*

WEEK FIFTEEN   *Finding God's Will*

WEEK SIXTEEN   *Avoiding Emotional Burn-out*

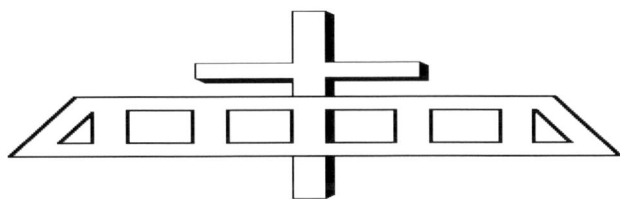

Having a poor self-image robs us of confidence. Confidence is a must if we are to build a healthy self-image. We are not referring to self-confidence here, but rather confidence that God loves us and places great value on us as a person--confidence that He will enable us to be successful as long as we work with Him. We will find satisfaction and fulfillment as we become familiar with His principles for success.

Week 14

What is Truly Worthwhile

Many of those in our society today suffer from poor self-image. The experts relate this problem to every ill imaginable; social, physical, mental and spiritual. It has been noted that to be successful, a good self-image is vital. We need to feel good about ourselves. Any therapist or counselor worth his salt will certainly pay close attention to this need when working with a patient.

It is in an attempt to solve this problem that the philosophy "I'm OK, You're OK" was developed. However, does trying to convince ourselves that we are all great people really solve the problem? Not in my experience. We may tell a person that he or she is a wonderful, special person, but even while we are talking they are thinking, "Boy, I sure have him fooled. If he only knew me the way I know me." It seems that we are constantly looking for new mental games that we can play to help us feel good about ourselves. This would be great if those games worked, but the fact is, they simply don't. Psyching ourselves up to believe we are really special is like launching mental hot air balloons to carry us soaring in the clouds only to send us crashing to earth as soon as someone or something bursts our balloon.

If we are to really feel good about ourselves and build a positive self-image, these two things are necessary.

1. *We must be able to discern our **true** value.*
2. *We must know that what we are accomplishing with our lives is truly **worthwhile**.*

FIRST, **what is our true value?** One of my favorite hobbies is woodworking. I love to build furniture. Often, after I have created a special piece, I ask my wife Jamae what she thinks it's worth. I have made a few that are really special to her that she considers priceless. But the truth is I can place any price on them I want.

God created us and He is the one who sets the true worth of man. Jesus asked the question, "What does it profit a man if he gains the whole world and loses his soul?" (Matthew 16:26) The implication is that the value Christ places on each of us is that we are worth more than the entire world. **Christ demonstrated our true worth to Him when He willingly gave His life to purchase us.**

The fact remains that without Christ we are spiritually dead. In that state we are of little worth; but once we have been made alive in Christ Jesus, we are priceless to God. I can feel good about myself because of my true worth in Jesus Christ.

SECOND, **we must know we are accomplishing something worthwhile with our lives.** This can only happen when we know that what we are doing has eternal significance. We must realize that the only thing eternal in this world is the souls of people. We are eternal beings. We will exist somewhere for all eternity -- either with God in the place He has prepared for those who have received eternal life, or in that place of eternal separation from Him, that place of punishment called hell. I have said this to stress the fact that anything really worthwhile in this life must be related to bringing people to Jesus and helping them prepare for eternity. We must learn to ask ourselves, "How does what I am doing right now relate to eternity?" The more things we bring into our lives that have eternal value, the better we will feel about ourselves.

We know that what we do here on earth has a bearing on our position and on our rewards in heaven, but preparing for eternity also has a tremendous effect on how we feel about ourselves here.

If we are to make doing what is worthwhile a priority in our lives, there are some areas that will need attention.

1. **We should heed what we fill our minds with.** I am thankful that, the first year after I became a Christian, I made reading God's Word a priority. The knowledge of God's Word that I gained that first year I still have, and I have tried to add to it over the years. I am very sure the quality of my life would have decreased had I not made spiritual wisdom and knowledge a priority in my life. Is filling your mind with God's Word a priority in your life? Do you enjoy spending time in prayer with Him?

2. **We need to give attention to those things we want to accomplish.** Knowledge of God and His Word will do us no good unless we put it to work. The principles we learn from the Bible should permeate all that we do. There are some practical aspects to investing in the eternal. In Acts 1, Jesus instructs us to be His witnesses and to share our faith with others. We are also told in Matthew 10 that when we minister in the name of a prophet (assist a prophet in his ministry), we will receive the same reward as

the prophet. Often **the first step to finding our own ministry is in helping others with theirs.**

3. **We should give heed to what we invest in.** In Matthew 6:21, Jesus tells us that what we treasure reveals where our heart is. He also teaches us that we can store up riches in heaven (Luke 12). The best investments I have made are in the Kingdom of God. Not only has the church been of incalculable benefit to my family and me but I will also benefit from the gifts I give. These benefits will last for eternity. Can you think of a better investment than that?

STUDY SHEET - WEEK 14

Memory Verse: "I can do all things through Christ who strengthens me." Philippians 4:13

DAYS 1-6:   Each day review the material for Week 14 in the manual.
Spend time with God in prayer then record a blessing received for the day.

Day 1   Reflection question: When you consider your self-worth, what emotions do you feel: guilt, jealousy, self-pity, satisfaction, confidence, etc.? Are these emotions healthy or unhealthy?
Additional study passage - Psalm 43:5

Day 2   Reflection question: What accomplishments or failures in your life have contributed to the value you place on yourself as a person? Please explain.
Additional study passage - Colossians 3:16-17

Day 3   Reflection question: Is there any one person who has shaped your estimate of your self-worth? If so, why is that person's estimate of you so important in your life?
Additional study passage – Matthew 15:25-28

Day 4   For Reflection: List some problems that may develop in our lives when we suffer from poor self-worth.
Additional study passage - Romans 2:1-2

Day 5   Reflection question: What are the goals that you have set for yourself? List several accomplishments you would consider truly worthwhile.
Additional study passage - I Thessalonians 1:3-4

Day 6   Reflection question: In order of priority, what do you consider the two most important things you could do to assist Christ in accomplishing His purpose in the world? Additional study passage - Luke 19:10

TO BE CONFIDENT

Week 15

Finding God's Will

The Bible says, *Do not be unwise, but understand what the will of the Lord is."* Ephesians 5:17.

It is certain that the only way we can be a real success is to fulfill God's will in our lives. And obviously the only way we can do His will is to know His will. God's Word instructs us to know His will. He will certainly make the knowledge of His will available to all His children.

The question I often hear, however, is **"How can I know the will of the Lord?" In this study, we will discover where to look when seeking direction for our lives.**

First*, let's look at the primary source of knowledge about God and His will for us.* We must have an anchor to keep us from drifting off course. We need something that is unchanging and can be depended upon to rightly relate God's goals, priorities, likes and dislikes. That reliable and unchanging document which shows us God's great plan, which He wishes each of us to be a part of, is the Bible, God's Word. Jesus tells us that nothing will change until all is complete (Matthew 5: 17-19). If we are to be successful in determining God's will, it is essential for us to have a good knowledge of God's Word.

After I received Christ, I had a burning desire to know His plan for my life. I spent hours each day reading my Bible, I read it through completely twice and some parts I read four and five times that first year. The more I absorbed the scriptures, the easier it became to know God's will. God will never lead us to violate the truths or purposes that are spelled out in His Word. I have known some to put more confidence in personal experiences, human reason, dreams, visions, etc. than in the Bible. If their personal revelation or dream disagrees with the Bible, too bad for God's Word. Anyone or any group that encourages this attitude is dangerous indeed. Read carefully Revelations 22:19. Jesus' words in Matthew 5 make it plain that the Bible refers to the whole of God's revelation to us. Your success at knowing and following the will of God for your life will be directly related to your ability to accept and absorb the truths in His Word.

The second key *in knowing God's will is found in Jesus Himself.* God's perfect will for our lives is not found in a place or a thing, but in a person -- Jesus Christ. We can't walk in God's will unless we are walking with Jesus.

Entering into God's perfect will occurs when we surrender our life to Jesus. The Bible term for this is "making Jesus our Lord." Making Him Lord is simply giving Him control of our lives. Giving Him control places us in the center of God's will for our lives. Any act of rebellion against Him takes us out of God's will.

The third essential *to walking in God's will is to understand the work of our spiritual guide, the Holy Spirit.* When He lives within us, we have His inner peace if we are doing what He would have us do. This peace is the key to walking in God's will. When we do not have God's peace, it is certain that we have ceased to walk in God's will. (John 14:27)

Let me share an example from my own life. When I accepted Christ at the age 26, I was working in Angola, Africa. Almost immediately, God began showing me that I was to enter into the ministry. Since I had spent the past two years in Africa, I just assumed that after my schooling was complete, God would want me back in Africa. However, Africa was not what I wanted for my life, so I told the Lord I would go anywhere but back to the "dark continent." That decision to control my own life destroyed the peace I had gained through my new relationship with Christ. I sensed that Christ was demanding complete surrender, but I was unwilling to give it. My prayer time suffered, as did my Bible study time. I was miserable. Finally, tired of the struggle, I apologized to the Lord. I had originally come to Africa with an oil company for the money. How small it was of me to refuse to go back to Africa that people might be saved!

God's immediate response was to assure me that He wasn't sending me to preach in Africa, but my desire to direct my own life was affecting my relationship with Him. My inner peace was restored, and that peace has become an important key in my life. That peace is testimony that God is pleased with my motives, attitudes and direction. It feels good to walk with Jesus.

The fourth essential *to walking in God's will is to spend time in prayer daily with Him.* Jesus made prayer a priority throughout His life here. He sought alone time with His Father during the times of greatest stress.

Just ask Jesus to teach you to pray. He said, "You have not because you do not ask." Remember when you are talking to Jesus, you're talking to a friend. And don't forget the Lord told us that the Holy Spirit is standing by to help with our prayers.

I continually stress prayer in my ministry, because I have observed that those who spend sufficient time in prayer daily are much easier to work with. They are less judgmental and critical of others, and they have a deeper capacity for love toward God and others.

STUDY SHEET - WEEK 15

Memory Verse: "Therefore, do not be unwise, but understand what the will of the Lord is." Ephesians 5:17

DAYS 1-6: Each day review the material for Week 15 in the manual.
Spend time with God in prayer then record a blessing received for the day.

Day 1 For Reflection: Give at least two good reasons why a person with a poor knowledge of God's Word will have trouble finding God's will.
Additional study passage - Psalm 119:103-105

Day 2 Reflection question: Make a list of the things that are most important in your life. On the list of priorities, where does the Bible fall? Is this verified by your faithfulness to read and study it?
Additional study passages - Isaiah 5:24-25

Day 3 For Reflection: Explain why God's will and complete surrender to Christ are synonymous.
Additional study passages - Matthew 12:30

Day 4 For Reflection: List any attitudes or controls in your life that would hinder you from being at peace with Christ.
Additional study passage - Isaiah 48:16-18

Day 5 Reflection question: The Holy Spirit already knows God's will for your life. If you are a child of God, the Holy Spirit lives within you. What is a sure sign that you are in the center of God's will for your life?
Additional study passage - John 14:25-27

Day 6 Reflection question: Is there any place you would be unwilling to go or anything you would be unwilling to do if God asked you? Is there something He is asking you to do that you haven't done?
Additional study passage - I Samuel 15: 22-23

Week 16

Avoiding Emotional Burn-out

EMOTIONAL ENERGY

God has designed our bodies so that we have a reservoir of emotional energy. This energy fuels our mind. Once we have depleted our reserves of this emotional energy, our mind's ability to function is impaired. The simplest tasks become difficult.

My first thought when I answered the phone and the caller identified himself was something is very wrong here. His speech was slurred, he had trouble forming his sentences, and there was strangeness in his voice I could not identify. I was immediately very concerned. He told me he had taken his wife to the hospital emergency room, she had been admitted and her condition was not good.

This was a man I had known for two years. He had come to the ministry from one of our churches to be an encourager for those in our program with addiction problems. I had been immediately impressed with his sharp clear mind. I needed his business knowledge in setting up SAFE Ministries. He was named president. He moved into the ministries home when we needed a director. He worked night and day helping addicts detox, directing our move into our new facilities, setting up our thrift store, helping with remodeling, directing a SAFE program in his church where he was associate pastor, and had many other responsibilities related to this fast-growing under staffed ministry.

During the time he was working so tirelessly with us there were untold other pressures on him. He underwent major back surgery, left a high paying executive job (with no promise of pay with us), had the motor in his car blow up, saw his pastor and friend resign to take a church in Arizona, and was asked to be interim pastor (later called as pastor) of his church. He also began a much needed remodeling project at this church. Each and every one of these things required huge amounts of emotional energy.

Two weeks before I received the disturbing call, while at our monthly board meeting, it became apparent that my friend was slipping. Simple problems had become difficult for him. He did not have enough emotional energy to fuel his sharp mind. I began trying to take some of his load; but he plowed ahead, and then I got the phone call. He knew things were not right. The next day he was still trying to push ahead even though his motor skills were impaired. His speech was worse, he couldn't hold his car keys, and he spilled his coffee more than once. We went out together in his car, and I was forced to drive. A lady he had never met before asked if he were retarded! He was plenty scared and confided that he was sure he had a brain tumor. This fear was a further drain. Things had gotten serious, so a trip to the neurologist was indicated. His neurologist ruled out a tumor in short order, and the diagnosis was emotional burn out. The cure was rest.

In the weeks that have followed it was great to watch the day-to- day recovery as my friend learned to pace himself and conserve his emotional energy.

AVOIDING EMOTIONAL BURN OUT

Strong emotions like fear and anger are a huge emotional drain. They short-circuit our emotions. Guilt, bitterness, etc. are a constant drain. Once these unhealthy emotions gain control in our lives, they strip us of the emotional energy that we need to live healthy, productive lives. Stimulants and depressants such as drugs and alcohol have the same disastrous effect.

We must learn to conserve this energy and use it in productive endeavors if we are to ever be the man/woman God intends us to be. Below are some suggestions on how you can make the best use of this emotional energy.

I. We must learn to conserve emotional energy. Energy drained by useless emotions [fear, lust, anger, guilt, worry, etc.] robs us of the ability to do our best mental work.

II. We should maintain a mental list of priorities. We must spend our energy on things that really count [the Lord, family, ministry, work, etc.] and not waste this precious energy on things that destroy our mental health and harm our fellowship with God.

III. Learn to draw energy from the Holy Spirit. God says, "not by power or by might but by my Spirit." When we are working with God to accomplish His purpose, we can draw from His Spirit. We can always accomplish more working with God than we ever could by ourselves.

WORKING WITH GOD - NOT FOR GOD

The wisest way to keep our emotional battery charged is to learn to work *with* God. Working *for* God we focus on **rules**. We work to please Him or to earn His favor. When working *with* God the **relationship** is primary. We are spiritually mature enough to realize that Christ is more interested in us, and what He can do for us, than what we can do for Him. Our work and labor for Him grows out of the fact that we are a part of Him and all that He is doing. We don't work *for* Him but *with* Him.

STUDY SHEET - WEEK 16

Memory Verse: "Let your conduct be without covetousness; be content with such things as you have. For He Himself has said, 'I will never leave you nor forsake you.'" Hebrews 13:5

DAYS 1-6:   Each day review the material for Week 16 in the manual.
Spend time with God in prayer then record a blessing received for the day.

Day 1   *Reflection Question*: List the two emotions upon which you expend the most emotional energy. Is this emotional drain productive or non-productive?
Additional study passage - Psalms 37:7-8

Day 2   *Reflection Question*: List two healthy goals you have for your life. Would gaining control of unhealthy emotions help you to realize these goals?
Additional study passage - Proverbs 15:13-15

Day 3   *Reflection Question*: List some activities in your life that cause an unhealthy drain on your emotions. What could you change about your lifestyle to help stop this waste of emotional energy?
Additional study passage - Proverbs 14:29-30

Day 4   *Reflection Question*: In developing a close personal relationship with Christ what activities require the expenditure of considerable emotional energy?
Additional study passage - Ecclesiastes 3:12-13

Day 5   *Reflection Question*: How can we promote an unhealthy drain of emotions in others? How can you help others conserve emotional energy?
Additional study passage – Philippians 2:1-4

Day 6   *Reflection Question*: Explain why conserving emotional energy will allow us to have more joy and peace in our lives.
Additional study passage - 1 Timothy 6:6-8

Week 17

Sabotaging Your Life

He has come so far since that day he came into my office. That day he learned for the first time what Jesus had done just for him and how much God loves him. I began watching his steady progress on his road to emotional stability. He has a good mind, but emotional instability had robbed him of the power to use it.

For two years he allowed God to work, putting his shattered life back together. I watched as once again, he began to dare to hope.

Today he had a troubled look in his eyes - there was fear there. "What are you afraid of," I asked. "Sabotage," he said. "I'm not used to doing so well, and I'm afraid I **will mess it all up.**"

In the days that followed I asked each person with whom I was counseling if they were concerned that they would sabotage their lives again. Without exception, the answer was always "YES!" I realized that I had overlooked a problem of great concern for those who are on the road to recovery and freedom from bondage.

Once a person is doing well, there is a tendency for that person to wreck the new life and return to the old. It was vital to find the answer to this problem. I was continually asking the questions, "Why would you deliberately sabotage your life, when you're doing so well? Why would you want to return to the life you had before?"From the answers I received and with God's guidance, I pieced together the information I will now share.

The first question we must answer is: "Why?"

I found that there were three reasons:

1. "I don't deserve a good life. I am no good."
2. "I haven't earned the good things I am receiving. I feel guilty taking them."
3. "I feel more comfor*table with the bad life that I am familiar with than I do with the* good life that I don't know how to relate to."

Let's address these attitudes that would rob us of the joy and peace that Christ has prepared for us. I strongly suspect that the culprit behind the attitudes is Satan himself.

ATTITUDE #1: **"I don't deserve the good life that Christ is offering me. I am not a good person, so I must punish myself."**

The root problem here is a poor self- image.

While it is true that, within ourselves, we are not good ("...there is none good but God...," Matthew 19:17), Christ brings His goodness when we invite Him into our lives. It is an insult to Christ when I seek to punish myself for my imperfection when He has already been punished for them. He certainly is not happy when I punish myself for something for which He has already suffered. What makes Him happy is for us to give all our imperfections to Him – for us to just get on with our lives, walking in obedience to Him. He certainly does not gain glory when I punish myself.

We must develop the attitude that we are complete and good in Him. We have value and purpose. Satan would steal from us our joy, peace and confidence. Don't let him have that victory.

ATTITUDE #2: **"I have not earned the blessing Christ is giving me."**

The root problem is pride.

The person with this attitude soon wearies of the guilt of receiving that which he hasn't earned. Usually the person who develops the attitude that he can't enjoy and appreciate that which they haven't earned is, by nature, a very sensitive person. Satan loves to twist things so that we cannot enjoy the good things God so freely gives His children.

When Christ blesses, His motive is not to make us feel guilty because we haven't earned it. His purpose is that we enjoy those blessings. When a young man brings his sweetheart flowers, he would be hurt if she refused them because she hadn't earned them. He has no desire that she work for them; he simply wants her thanks (and maybe a kiss).

We can never earn even the smallest of God's blessings. He knows that. He doesn't expect it of us. He simply wants us to love Him, thank Him, and do our best to be obedient to Him. I am so glad I don't have to earn the wonderful things God gives me.

ATTITUDE #3: **"It is easier to return to an unhealthy lifestyle that I am familiar with rather than to stay with the much better life that I have trouble relating to."**
The root problem here is fear.

It is true that we resist change. If this were not so, it would be really difficult to get to know a person. If that person were always changing, it would be hard to relate to that person.

We tend to fall into patterns of living and remain there. The Bible says God is the same yesterday, today and forever. **He is unchanging. We are made in His image** and change is hard for us. We tend to get locked in. We are creatures of habit -- it's hard for us to quit old habits and equally hard to form new ones. However, after we have forced ourselves into a new pattern of living and have mentally accepted the benefits of this new way of living, the strange becomes familiar, and soon we are just as entrenched in our new pattern as we were in our old.

After a period of time, we lose all desire to go back. My life was totally changed by 13 long weeks of Marine Corps boot camp. Many of the habits I was forced to accept are still a part of my life today.

So what do we do? We stay with it until we are comfortable in our new life Christ has prepared for us.

When I came to the Northwest 41 years ago, I realized the benefits of living in this beautiful area. But I was not comfortable. At first I had trouble relating to the people, their attitudes and their lifestyles. Now, after 41 years, I am more comfortable in Oregon than any other place on earth. I feel more at home here than I do in my native state of Mississippi.

Don't give up. Don't turn back. Life just gets better and better in the Lord. Just learn to enjoy and appreciate this wonderful new life Christ has prepared just for you.

STUDY SHEET - WEEK 17

Memory Verse: "But godliness with contentment is great gain."
                        I Timothy 6:6

DAYS 1-6:   Each day review the material for Week 17 in the manual.
                        Spend time with God in prayer then record a blessing received for the day.

Day 1   Reflection question: Why would you deliberately sabotage your life, when you're doing well? Why would you want to return to the life you had before?
                        Additional study passage - Philippians 4:4-8

Day 2   Reflection question: What do you think God expects of you that you are unable to give Him or do for Him?
                        Additional study passage - Micah 6:8

Day 3   For Reflection: List ways you consciously make your life difficult. Do you think these actions could be self- punishment or self-imposed penance?
                        Additional study passage - I Thessalonians 5:9-11

Day 4   Reflection question: Do you have trouble receiving gifts? When someone gives you a gift simply because they care for you, how do you respond?
                        Additional study passage - I Thessalonians 5:17-18

Day 5   Reflection question: How many major changes have occurred in your life? Were these changes forced or voluntary? How long did it take you to feel comfortable with the changes?
                        Additional study passage - Jeremiah 31:33-34

Day 6   Reflection question: God has a wonderful life planned for you. Are you willing to cling to Him long enough to adjust to this new life? What are some things you can do to shorten the adjustment period?
                        Additional study passage - Colossians 2:6-7

WEEKLY SELF EVALUATION WORKSHEET

name_____ date _____
Give yourself a score (0 to 10) related to how well you are doing in the categories listed.

ATTITUDE   [ ]

AUTHORITY ISSUES   [ ]

PERSONAL TIME WITH THE LORD   [ ]

RESPONSIBILITIES   [ ]

COMMITMENTS   [ ]

EMOTIONS

> **ANGER**   [ ]
> **GUILT**   [ ]
> **FEAR**   [ ]
> **RESENTMENTS**   [ ]
> **WORRIES**   [ ]
> **PRIDE**   [ ]

comments:

Client's signature _____

encouragers notes:

Encourager's signature _____

Accountability Record

SAFE EXERCISES	Monday	Tuesday	Wednesday	Thursday	Friday	Saturday
SATURATION VERSE _____	MORE ☐ 100 ☐ LESS ☐	MORE ☐ 100 ☐ LESS ☐	MORE ☐ 100 ☐ LESS ☐	MORE ☐ 100 ☐ LESS ☐	MORE ☐ 100 ☐ LESS ☐	MORE ☐ 100 ☐ LESS ☐
BIBLE READING	CHAPTERS _____	CHAPTERS _____	CHAPTERS _____	CHAPTERS _____	CHAPTERS _____	CHAPTERS _____
SAFE MANUAL LESSON # _____	READ TODAY'S LESSON TODAY YES ☐ NO ☐	READ TODAY'S LESSON TODAY YES ☐ NO ☐	READ TODAY'S LESSON TODAY YES ☐ NO ☐	READ TODAY'S LESSON TODAY YES ☐ NO ☐	READ TODAY'S LESSON TODAY YES ☐ NO ☐	READ TODAY'S LESSON TODAY YES ☐ NO ☐
REFLECTION QUESTION	COMPLETED TODAY'S LESSON TODAY YES ☐ NO ☐	COMPLETED TODAY'S LESSON TODAY YES ☐ NO ☐	COMPLETED TODAY'S LESSON TODAY YES ☐ NO ☐	COMPLETED TODAY'S LESSON TODAY YES ☐ NO ☐	COMPLETED TODAY'S LESSON TODAY YES ☐ NO ☐	COMPLETED TODAY'S LESSON TODAY YES ☐ NO ☐
PRIVATE PRAYER	TIME SPENT _____	TIME SPENT _____	TIME SPENT _____	TIME SPENT _____	TIME SPENT _____	TIME SPENT _____
TODAY I AM THANKFUL FOR						

SAFE ZONE CHART

GRANDIOSE

EGOTISTICAL

PROUD

IRATE

ARROGANT

ANGRY

BOASTFUL

SELF-RIGHTEOUS

LOVING

PEACEFUL

CARING

JOYFUL

HOPEFUL

SAFE ZONE

KIND

TRUSTFUL

CONFIDENT

FORGIVING

PARANOID

Dejected

Sorrowful

ANGRY

Morbid

Depressed

Negative

GUILT-RIDDEN

Faultfinding

Bitter

Afraid

Addendum:

THE ADDITIONAL STUDY PASSAGES
for
The Transformation Principle

WEEK 1

D1

2 Corinthians 10:3 For though we walk in the flesh, we do not war according to the flesh. 4 For the weapons of our warfare are not carnal but mighty in God for pulling down strongholds, 5 casting down arguments and every high thing that exalts itself against the knowledge of God, bringing every thought into captivity to the obedience of Christ, 6 and being ready to punish all disobedience when your obedience is fulfilled.

D2

Psalms 15:1 A Psalm of David. LORD, who may abide in Your tabernacle? Who may dwell in Your holy hill? 2 He who walks uprightly, And works righteousness, And speaks the truth in his heart; 3 He who does not backbite with his tongue, Nor does evil to his neighbor, Nor does he take up a reproach against his friend; 4 In whose eyes a vile person is despised, But he honors those who fear the LORD; He who swears to his own hurt and does not change; 5 He who does not put out his money at usury, Nor does he take a bribe against the innocent. He who does these things shall never be moved.

D3

Colossians 3:13 bearing with one another, and forgiving one another, if anyone has a complaint against another; even as Christ forgave you, so you also must do.14 But above all these things put on love, which is the bond of perfection. 15 And let the peace of God rule in your hearts, to which also you were called in one body; and be thankful.16 Let the word of Christ dwell in you richly in all wisdom, teaching and admonishing one another in psalms and hymns and spiritual songs, singing with grace in your hearts to the Lord. 7 And whatever you do in word or deed, do all in the name of the Lord Jesus, giving thanks to God the Father through Him.

D4

John 5:39 You search the Scriptures, for in them you think you have eternal life; and these are they which testify of Me.

D5

Mark 4:26 And He said, "The kingdom of God is as if a man should scatter seed on the ground, 27 and should sleep by night and rise by day, and the seed should sprout and grow, he himself does not know how. 28 For the earth yields crops by itself: first the blade, then the head, after that the full grain in the head. 29 But when the grain ripens, immediately he puts in the sickle, because the harvest has come." 30 Then He said, "To what shall we liken the kingdom of God? Or with what parable shall we picture it? 31 It is like a mustard seed which, when it is sown on the ground, is smaller than all the seeds on earth; 32 but when it is sown, it grows up and becomes greater than all herbs, and shoots out large branches, so that the birds of the air may nest under its shade."

D6

Philippians 4:8 Finally, brethren, whatever things are true, whatever things are noble, whatever things are just, whatever things are pure, whatever things are lovely, whatever things are of good report, if there is any virtue and if there is anything praiseworthy—meditate on these things.

WEEK 2

D1

1 Corinthians 3:11 For no other foundation can anyone lay than that which is laid, which is Jesus Christ. 12 Now if anyone builds on this foundation with gold, silver, precious stones, wood, hay, straw, 13 each one's work will become clear; for the Day will declare it, because it will be revealed by fire; and the fire will test each one's work, of what sort it is. 14 If anyone's work which he has built on it endures, he will receive a reward. 15 If anyone's work is burned, he will suffer loss; but he himself will be saved, yet so as through fire.

D2

Revelations 21:1 Now I saw a new heaven and a new earth, for the first heaven and the first earth had passed away. Also there was no more sea. 2 Then I, John, saw the holy city, New Jerusalem, coming down out of heaven from God, prepared as a bride adorned for her husband. 3 And I heard a loud voice from heaven saying, "Behold, the tabernacle of God is with men, and He will dwell with them, and they shall be His people. God Himself will be with them and be their God. 4 And God will wipe away every tear from their eyes; there shall be no more death, nor sorrow, nor crying. There shall be no more pain, for the former things have passed away." 5 Then He who sat on the throne said, "Behold, I make all things new." And He said to me, "Write, for these words are true and faithful."

D3

2 Corinthians 7:9 Now I rejoice, not that you were made sorry, but that your sorrow led to repentance. For you were made sorry in a godly manner, that you might suffer loss from us in nothing. 10 For godly sorrow produces repentance leading to salvation, not to be regretted; but the sorrow of the world produces death.

D4

1 Peter 3:15 But sanctify the Lord God in your hearts, and always be ready to give a defense to everyone who asks you a reason for the hope that is in you, with meekness and fear; 16 having a good conscience, that when they defame you as evildoers, those who revile your good conduct in Christ may be ashamed.

D5

John 1:1 In the beginning was the Word, and the Word was with God, and the Word was God. 2 He was in the beginning with God. 3 All things were made through Him, and without Him nothing was made that was made. 4 In Him was life, and the life was the light of men. 5 And the light shines in the darkness, and the darkness did not comprehend it. 6 There was a man sent from God, whose name was John. 7 This man came for a witness, to bear witness of the Light, that all through him might believe. 8 He was not that Light, but was sent to bear witness of that Light. 9 That was the true Light which gives light to every man coming into the world. 10 He was in the world, and the world was made through Him, and the world did not know Him. 11 He came to His own, and His own did not receive Him. 12 But as many as received Him, to them He gave the right to become children of God, to those who believe in His name: 13 who were born, not of blood, nor of the will of the flesh, nor of the will of man, but of God.

D6

Ephesians 5:8 For you were once darkness, but now you are light in the Lord. Walk as children of light 9 (for the fruit of the Spirit is in all goodness, righteousness, and truth), 10 finding out what is acceptable to the Lord. 11 And have no fellowship with the unfruitful works of darkness, but rather expose them. 12 For it is shameful even to speak of those things which are done by them in secret. 13 But all things that are exposed are made manifest by the light, for whatever makes manifest is light. 14 Therefore He says: "Awake, you who sleep, Arise from the dead, And Christ will give you light."

WEEK 3

D1

Philippians 2:12 Therefore, my beloved, as you have always obeyed, not as in my presence only, but now much more in my absence, work out your own salvation with fear and trembling; 13 for it is God who works in you both to will and to do for His good pleasure. 14 Do all things without complaining and disputing, 15 that you may become blameless and harmless, children of God without fault in the midst of a crooked and perverse generation, among whom you shine as lights in the world, 16 holding fast the word of life, so that I may rejoice in the day of Christ that I have not run in vain or labored in vain.

D2

James 3:13 Who is wise and understanding among you? Let him show by good conduct that his works are done in the meekness of wisdom. 14 But if you have bitter envy and self-seeking in your hearts, do not boast and lie against the truth. 15 This wisdom does not descend from above, but is earthly, sensual, demonic. 16 For where envy and self-seeking exist, confusion and every evil thing are there. 17 But the wisdom that is from above is first pure, then peaceable, gentle, willing to yield, full of mercy and good fruits, without partiality and without hypocrisy.18 Now the fruit of righteousness is sown in peace by those who make peace.

D3

Philippians 3:12 Not that I have already attained, or am already perfected; but I press on, that I may lay hold of that for which Christ Jesus has also laid hold of me. 13 Brethren, I do not count myself to have apprehended; but one thing I do, forgetting those things which are behind and reaching forward to those things which are ahead, 14 I press toward the goal for the prize of the upward call of God in Christ Jesus. 15 Therefore let us, as many as are mature, have this mind; and if in anything you think otherwise, God will reveal even this to you.

D4

Mark 4:14 The sower sows the word. 15 And these are the ones by the wayside where the word is sown. When they hear, Satan comes immediately and takes away the word that was sown in their hearts. 16 These likewise are the ones sown on stony ground who, when they hear the word, immediately receive it with gladness; 17 and they have no root in themselves, and so endure only for a time. Afterward, when tribulation or persecution arises for the word's sake, immediately they stumble. 18 Now these are the ones sown among thorns; they are the ones who hear the word, 19 and the cares of this world, the deceitfulness of riches, and the desires for other things entering in choke the word, and it becomes unfruitful. 20 But these are the ones sown on good ground, those who hear the word, accept it, and bear fruit: some thirtyfold, some sixty, and some a hundred."

D5

Psalms 25:12 Who is the man that fears the LORD? Him shall He teach in the way He chooses. 13 He himself shall dwell in prosperity, And his descendants shall inherit the earth. 14 The secret of the LORD is with those who fear Him, and He will show them His covenant. 15 My eyes are ever toward the LORD, For He shall pluck my feet out of the net.

D6

Psalms 63:1 A Psalm of David When He Was in the Wilderness of Judah. O God, You are my God; Early will I seek You; My soul thirsts for You; My flesh longs for You In a dry and thirsty land Where there is no water. 2 So I have looked for You in the sanctuary, To see Your power and Your glory. 3 Because Your lovingkindness is better than life, My lips shall praise You. 4 Thus I will bless You while I live; I will lift up my hands in Your name. 5 My soul shall be satisfied as with marrow and fatness, And my mouth shall praise You with joyful lips.

WEEK 4

D1

John 6:44 No one can come to Me unless the Father who sent Me draws him; and I will raise him up at the last day.

12:32 And I, if I am lifted up from the earth, will draw all peoplesto Myself."

D2

Psalms 118:8 It is better to trust in the LORD Than to put confidence in man. 9 It is better to trust in the LORD Than to put confidence in princes.

D3 Jeremiah 17:7 "Blessed is the man who trusts in the LORD, And whose hope is the LORD.
8 For he shall be like a tree planted by the waters, Which spreads out its roots by the river, And will not fear when heat comes; But its leaf will be green, And will not be anxious in the year of drought, Nor will cease from yielding fruit.

D4

2 Timothy 2:22 Flee also youthful lusts; but pursue righteousness, faith, love, peace with those who call on the Lord out of a pure heart.23 But avoid foolish and ignorant disputes, knowing that they generate strife. 24 And a servant of the Lord must not quarrel but be gentle to all, able to teach, patient, 25 in humility correcting those who are in opposition, if God perhaps will grant them repentance, so that they may know the truth, 26 and that they may come to their senses and escapethe snare of the devil, having been taken captive by him to do his will.

D5

Galatians 3:1 O foolish Galatians! Who has bewitched you that you should not obey the truth, before whose eyes Jesus Christ was clearly portrayed among you as crucified? 2 This only I want to learn from you: Did you receive the Spirit by the works of the law, or by the hearing of faith?— 3 Are you so foolish? Having begun in the Spirit, are you now being made perfect by the flesh? 4 Have you suffered so many things in vain—if indeed it was in vain? 5 Therefore He who supplies the Spirit to you and works miracles among you, does He do itby the works of the law, or by the hearing of faith? 6 just as Abraham "BELIEVED GOD, AND IT WAS ACCOUNTED TO HIM FOR

RIGHTEOUSNESS." 7 Therefore know that only those who are of faith are sons of Abraham.

D6

1 Thessalonians 5:8 But let us who are of the day be sober, putting on the breastplate of faith and love, and as a helmet the hope of salvation. 9 For God did not appoint us to wrath, but to obtain salvation through our Lord Jesus Christ, 10 who died for us, that whether we wake or sleep, we should live together with Him. 11 Therefore comfort each other and edify one another, just as you also are doing.

WEEK 5

D1

Isaiah 32:15 Until the Spirit is poured upon us from on high, And the wilderness becomes a fruitful field, And the fruitful field is counted as a forest. 16 Then justice will dwell in the wilderness, And righteousness remain in the fruitful field. 17 The work of righteousness will be peace, And the effect of righteousness, quietness and assurance forever. 18 My people will dwell in a peaceful habitation, In secure dwellings, and in quiet resting places, 19 Though hail comes down on the forest, And the city is brought low in humiliation.

D2

Isaiah 57:19 "I create the fruit of the lips: Peace, peace to him who isfar off and to him who is near," Says the LORD, "And I will heal him." 20 But the wicked are like the troubled sea, When it cannot rest, Whose waters cast up mire and dirt. 21 "There isno peace," Says my God, "for the wicked."

D3

Hebrew 4:1 Therefore, since a promise remains of entering His rest, let us fear lest any of you seem to have come short of it. 2 For indeed the gospel was preached to us as well as to them; but the word which they heard did not profit them, not being mixed with faith in those who heard it.

D4

Mark 6:30 Then the apostles gathered to Jesus and told Him all things, both what they had done and what they had taught. 31 And He said to them, "Come aside by yourselves to a deserted place and rest a while." For there were many coming and going, and they did not even have time to eat. 32 So they departed to a deserted place in the boat by themselves.

D5

Psalms 120:6 My soul has dwelt too long with one who hates peace.

7 I am for peace; but when I speak, they are for war.

D6

Philippians 4:4 Rejoice in the Lord always. Again I will say, rejoice! 5 Let your gentleness be known to all men. The Lord is at hand. 6 Be anxious for nothing, but in everything by prayer and supplication, with thanksgiving, let your requests be made known to God; 7 and the peace of God, which surpasses all understanding, will guard your hearts and minds through Christ Jesus.

WEEK6

D1

2 Chronicles 14:11 And Asa cried out to the LORD his God, and said, "LORD, it is nothing for You to help, whether with many or with those who have no power; help us, O LORD our God, for we

rest on You, and in Your name we go against this multitude. O LORD, You are our God; do not let man prevail against You!" 12 So the LORD struck the Ethiopians before Asa and Judah, and the Ethiopians fled.

D2

Romans 15:13 Now may the God of hope fill you with all joy and peace in believing, that you may abound in hope by the power of the Holy Spirit.

D3

Habbakuk 2:4 "Behold the proud, his soul is not upright in him; but the just shall live by his faith.

D4

1 Corinthians 15:33 Do not be deceived: "Evil company corrupts good habits." 34 Awake to righteousness, and do not sin; for some do not have the knowledge of God. I speak this to your shame.

D5

1 Corinthians 2:3 I was with you in weakness, in fear, and in much trembling. 4 And my speech and my preaching were not with persuasive words of human wisdom, but in demonstration of the Spirit and of power, 5 that your faith should not be in the wisdom of men but in the power of God.

D6

Romans 10:16 But they have not all obeyed the gospel. For Isaiah says, "LORD, WHO HAS BELIEVED OUR REPORT?" 17 So then faith comes by hearing, and hearing by the word of God.

WEEK 7

D1

2 Corinthians 10:3 For though we walk in the flesh, we do not war according to the flesh. 4 For the weapons of our warfare are not carnal but mighty in God for pulling down strongholds, 5 casting down arguments and every high thing that exalts itself against the knowledge of God, bringing every thought into captivity to the obedience of Christ, 6 and being ready to punish all disobedience when your obedience is fulfilled.

D2

Matthew 15:17 Do you not yet understand that whatever enters the mouth goes into the stomach and is eliminated? 18 But those things which proceed out of the mouth come from the heart, and they defile a man. 19 For out of the heart proceed evil thoughts, murders, adulteries, fornications, thefts, false witness, blasphemies. 20 These are the things which defile a man, but to eat with unwashed hands does not defile a man."

D3

Philippians 4:6 Be anxious for nothing, but in everything by prayer and supplication, with thanksgiving, let your requests be made known to God; 7 and the peace of God, which surpasses all understanding, will guard your hearts and minds through Christ Jesus. 8 Finally, brethren, whatever things are true, whatever things are noble, whatever things are just, whatever things are pure, whatever things are lovely, whatever things are of good report, if there is any virtue and if there is anything praiseworthy—meditate on these things.

D4

Hebrews 4:9 There remains therefore a rest for the people of God. 10 For he who has entered

His rest has himself also ceased from his works as God did from His. 11 Let us therefore be diligent to enter that rest, lest anyone fall according to the same example of disobedience. 12 For the word of God is living and powerful, and sharper than any two-edged sword, piercing even to the division of soul and spirit, and of joints and marrow, and is a discerner of the thoughts and intents of the heart.

D5

Ezekiel 11:19 Then I will give them one heart, and I will put a new spirit within them, and take the stony heart out of their flesh, and give them a heart of flesh, 20 that they may walk in My statutes and keep My judgments and do them; and they shall be My people, and I will be their God. 21 But as for those whose hearts follow the desire for their detestable things and their abominations, I will recompense their deeds on their own heads," says the Lord GOD

D6

Psalms 119:28 My soul melts from heaviness; strengthen me according to Your word. 29 Remove from me the way of lying, And grant me Your law graciously 30 I have chosen the way of truth; Your judgments I have laid before me.31 I cling to Your testimonies; O LORD, do not put me to shame!

WEEK 8

D1

Ezekiel 18:30 "Therefore I will judge you, O house of Israel, every one according to his ways," says the Lord GOD. "Repent, and turn from all your transgressions, so that iniquity will not be your ruin. :31 Cast away from you all the transgressions which you have committed, and get yourselves a new heart and a new spirit. For why should you die, O house of Israel? 32 For I have no pleasure in the death of one who dies," says the Lord GOD. "Therefore turn and live!"

D2

Deuteronomy 23:21 "When you make a vow to the LORD your God, you shall not delay to pay it; for the LORD your God will surely require it of you, and it would be sin to you. 22 But if you abstain from vowing, it shall not be sin to you. 23 That which has gone from your lips you shall keep and perform, for you voluntarily vowed to the LORD your God what you have promised with your mouth.

D3

Luke 8:38 Now the man from whom the demons had departed begged Him that he might be with Him. But Jesus sent him away, saying, 39 "Return to your own house, and tell what great things God has done for you." And he went his way and proclaimed throughout the whole city what great things Jesus had done for him.

D4

Genesis 3:9 Then the LORD God called to Adam and said to him, "Where are you?" 10 So he said, "I heard Your voice in the garden, and I was afraid because I was naked; and I hid myself." 11 And He said, "Who told you that you were naked? Have you eaten from the tree of which I commanded you that you should not eat?" 12 Then the man said, "The woman whom You gave to be with me, she gave me of the tree, and I ate." 13 And the LORD God said to the woman, "What is this you have done?" The woman said, "The serpent deceived me, and I ate."

D5

John 1:11 He came to His own, and His own did not receive Him. 12 But as many as received Him, to them He gave the right to become children of God, to those who believe in His name: 13 who were born, not of blood, nor of the will of the flesh, nor of the will of man, but of God.

D6

Psalms 1:1 Blessed is the man Who walks not in the counsel of the ungodly, nor stands in the path of sinners, nor sits in the seat of the scornful; 2 but his delight is in the law of the LORD, and in His law he meditates day and night. 3 He shall be like a tree planted by the rivers of water, that brings forth its fruit in its season, whose leaf also shall not wither; and whatever he does shall prosper.

WEEK 9

D1

Psalms 138:7 Though I walk in the midst of trouble, You will revive me; You will stretch out Your hand against the wrath of my enemies, And Your right hand will save me. 8 The LORD will perfect that which concerns me; Your mercy, O LORD, endures forever; do not forsake the works of Your hands.

D2

Psalms 142:1 I cry out to the LORD with my voice; with my voice to the LORD I make my supplication. 2 I pour out my complaint before Him; I declare before Him my trouble. 3 When my spirit was overwhelmed within me, then You knew my path. In the way in which I walk they have secretly set a snare for me. 4 Look on my right hand and see, for there is no one who acknowledges me; refuge has failed me; no one cares for my soul. 5 I cried out to You, O LORD: I said, "You are my refuge, my portion in the land of the living. 6 Attend to my cry, for I am brought very low; deliver me from my persecutors, for they are stronger than I. 7 Bring my soul out of prison, that I may praise Your name; the righteous shall surround me, for You shall deal bountifully with me."

D3

Philippians 4:6 Be anxious for nothing, but in everything by prayer and supplication, with thanksgiving, let your requests be made known to God; 7 and the peace of God, which surpasses all understanding, will guard your hearts and minds through Christ Jesus.

D4

2 Corinthians 4:16 Therefore we do not lose heart. Even though our outward man is perishing, yet the inward man is being renewed day by day. 17 For our light affliction, which is but for a moment, is working for us a far more exceeding and eternal weight of glory, 18 while we do not look at the things which are seen, but at the things which are not seen. For the things which are seen are temporary, but the things which are not seen are eternal.

D5

Jonah 1:7 And they said to one another, "Come, let us cast lots, that we may know for whose cause this trouble has come upon us." So they cast lots, and the lot fell on Jonah. 8 Then they said to him, "Please tell us! For whose cause is this trouble upon us? What is your occupation? And where do you come from? What is your country? And of what people are you?" 9 So he said to them, "I am a Hebrew; and I fear the LORD, the God of heaven, who made the sea and the dry land." 10 Then the men were exceedingly afraid, and said to him, "Why have you done this?" For the men knew that he fled from the presence of the LORD, because he had told them. 11 Then they said to him, "What shall we do to you that the sea may be calm for us?"—for the sea was growing more tempestuous. 12 And he said to them, "Pick me up and throw me into the sea; then the sea will become calm for you. For I know that this great tempest is because of me."

D6

Joshua 1:9 Have I not commanded you? Be strong and of good courage; do not be afraid, nor be dismayed, for the LORD your God is with you wherever you go."

WEEK 10

D1

1 Kings 18:21 And Elijah came to all the people, and said, "How long will you falter between two opinions? If the LORD is God, follow Him; but if Baal, follow him." But the people answered him not a word.

D2

Deuteronomy 30:15 "See, I have set before you today life and good, death and evil, 16 in that I command you today to love the LORD your God, to walk in His ways, and to keep His commandments, His statutes, and His judgments, that you may live and multiply; and the LORD your God will bless you in the land which you go to possess.

D3

Isaiah 14:12 "How you are fallen from heaven, O Lucifer, son of the morning! How you are cut down to the ground, You who weakened the nations! 13 For you have said in your heart: 'I will ascend into heaven, I will exalt my throne above the stars of God; I will also sit on the mount of the congregation On the farthest sides of the north; 14 I will ascend above the heights of the clouds, I will be like the Most High.'

D4

John 15:13 Greater love has no one than this, than to lay down one's life for his friends. 14 You are My friends if you do whatever I command you.

D5

1 Samuel 15:18 Now the LORD sent you on a mission, and said, 'Go, and utterly destroy the sinners, the Amalekites, and fight against them until they are consumed.' 19 Why then did you not obey the voice of the LORD? Why did you swoop down on the spoil, and do evil in the sight of the LORD?" 20 And Saul said to Samuel, "But I have obeyed the voice of the LORD, and gone on the mission on which the LORD sent me, and brought back Agag king of Amalek; I have utterly destroyed the Amalekites. 21 But the people took of the plunder, sheep and oxen, the best of the things which should have been utterly destroyed, to sacrifice to the LORD your God in Gilgal." 22 So Samuel said: "Has the LORD as great delight in burnt offerings and sacrifices, As in obeying the voice of the LORD? Behold, to obey is better than sacrifice, And to heed than the fat of rams.

D6

Joshua 1:7 Only be strong and very courageous, that you may observe to do according to all the law which Moses My servant commanded you; do not turn from it to the right hand or to the left, that you may prosper wherever you go. 8 This Book of the Law shall not depart from your mouth, but you shall meditate in it day and night, that you may observe to do according to all that is written in it. For then you will make your way prosperous, and then you will have good success.

WEEK 11

D1

1 Timothy 1:12 And I thank Christ Jesus our Lord who has enabled me, because He counted me faithful, putting me into the ministry, 13 although I was formerly a blasphemer, a persecutor, and an insolent man; but I obtained mercy because I did it ignorantly in unbelief.

D2

Psalms 15:3 He who does not backbite with his tongue, nor does evil to his neighbor, Nor does he take up a reproach against his friend;

Proverbs 17:17 A friend loves at all times, And a brother is born for adversity.

D3

James 4:4 Adulterers and adulteresses! Do you not know that friendship with the world is enmity with God? Whoever therefore wants to be a friend of the world makes himself an enemy of God. 5 Or do you think that the Scripture says in vain, "The Spirit who dwells in us yearns jealously"? 6 But He gives more grace. Therefore He says: "GOD RESISTS THE PROUD, BUT GIVES GRACE TO THE HUMBLE." 7 Therefore submit to God. Resist the devil and he will flee from you. 8 Draw near to God and He will draw near to you. Cleanse your hands, you sinners; and purify your hearts, you double-minded.

D4

Proverbs 18:24 A man who has friends must himself be friendly, But there is a friend who sticks closer than a brother.

D5

John 14:18 I will not leave you orphans; I will come to you. 19 "A little while longer and the world will see Me no more, but you will see Me. Because I live, you will live also. 20 At that day you will know that I am in My Father, and you in Me, and I in you.

D6

1 Peter 5:5 Likewise you younger people, submit yourselves to your elders. Yes, all of you be submissive to one another, and be clothed with humility, for "GOD RESISTS THE PROUD, BUT GIVES GRACE TO THE HUMBLE." 6 Therefore humble yourselves under the mighty hand of God, that He may exalt you in due time, 7 casting all your care upon Him, for He cares for you.

WEEK 12

D1

Psalms 37:7 Rest in the LORD, and wait patiently for Him; Do not fret because of him who prospers in his way, Because of the man who brings wicked schemes to pass. 8 Cease from anger, and forsake wrath; Do not fret—it only causes harm.

D2

Act 8:18 And when Simon saw that through the laying on of the apostles' hands the Holy Spirit was given, he offered them money, 19 saying, "Give me this power also, that anyone on whom I lay hands may receive the Holy Spirit." 20 But Peter said to him, "Your money perish with you, because you thought that the gift of God could be purchased with money! 21 You have neither part nor portion in this matter, for your heart is not right in the sight of God. 22 Repent therefore of this your wickedness, and pray God if perhaps the thought of your heart may be forgiven you. 23 For I see that you are poisoned by bitterness and bound by iniquity."

D3

Proverbs 10:12 Hatred stirs up strife, But love covers all sinsProverbs

Proverbs 10:18 Whoever hides hatred has lying lips, and whoever spreads slander is a fool.

D4

Rev 2:3 and you have persevered and have patience, and have labored for My name's sake and have not become weary. 4 Nevertheless I have this against you, that you have left your first love.

D5

John 8:34 Jesus answered them, "Most assuredly, I say to you, whoever commits sin is a slave of sin. 35 And a slave does not abide in the house forever, but a son abides forever. 36 Therefore if the Son makes you free, you shall be free indeed.

D6

1 Corinthians 13:3 And though I bestow all my goods to feed the poor, and though I give my body to be burned, but have not love, it profits me nothing. 4 Love suffers long and is kind; love does not envy; love does not parade itself, is not puffed up; 5 does not behave rudely, does not seek its own, is not provoked, thinks no evil; 6 does not rejoice in iniquity, but rejoices in the truth; 7 bears all things, believes all things, hopes all things, endures all things. 8 Love never fails. But whether there areprophecies, they will fail; whether there aretongues, they will cease; whether there isknowledge, it will vanish away.

WEEK 13

D1

Ephesians 4:26 "BE ANGRY, AND DO NOT SIN": do not let the sun go down on your wrath, 27 nor give place to the devil. 28 Let him who stole steal no longer, but rather let him labor, working with his hands what is good, that he may have something to give him who has need. 29 Let no corrupt word proceed out of your mouth, but what is good for necessary edification, that it may impart grace to the hearers. 30 And do not grieve the Holy Spirit of God, by whom you were sealed for the day of redemption. 31 Let all bitterness, wrath, anger, clamor, and evil speaking be put away from you, with all malice. 32 And be kind to one another, tenderhearted, forgiving one another, even as God in Christ forgave you.

D2

Colossians 2:6 As you therefore have received Christ Jesus the Lord, so walk in Him, 7 rooted and built up in Him and established in the faith, as you have been taught, abounding in it with thanksgiving. 8 Beware lest anyone cheat you through philosophy and empty deceit, according to the tradition of men, according to the basic principles of the world, and not according to Christ. 9 For in Him dwells all the fullness of the Godhead bodily; 10 and you are complete in Him, who is the head of all principality and power.

D3

Proverbs 27:1 Do not boast about tomorrow, For you do not know what a day may bring forth. 2 Let another man praise you, and not your own mouth; A stranger, and not your own lips. 3 A stone is heavy and sand is weighty, But a fool's wrath is heavier than both of them. 4 Wrath is cruel and anger a torrent, But who is able to stand before jealousy?

D4

Colossians 3:12 Therefore, as the elect of God, holy and beloved, put on tender mercies, kindness, humility, meekness, longsuffering; 13 bearing with one another, and forgiving one another, if anyone has a complaint against another; even as Christ forgave you, so you also must do. 14 But above all these things put on love, which is the bond of perfection. 15 And let the peace of God rule in your hearts, to which also you were called in one body; and be thankful.

D5

Proverbs 21:7 The violence of the wicked will destroy them, Because they refuse to do justice. 8 The way of a guilty man is perverse; but as for the pure, his work is right. 9 Better to dwell in a corner of a housetop, than in a house shared with a contentious woman.

D6

James 1:19-20 So then, my beloved brethren, let every man be swift to hear, slow to speak, slow to wrath; 20 for the wrath of man does not produce the righteousness of God.

WEEK 14

D1

Psalms 43:5 Why are you cast down, O my soul? And why are you disquieted within me? Hope in God; For I shall yet praise Him, The help of my countenance and my God.

D2

Colossians 3:16 Let the word of Christ dwell in you richly in all wisdom, teaching and admonishing one another in psalms and hymns and spiritual songs, singing with grace in your hearts to the Lord. 17 And whatever you do in word or deed, do all in the name of the Lord Jesus, giving thanks to God the Father through Him.

D3

Matthew 15:25 Then she came and worshiped Him, saying, "Lord, help me!" 26 But He answered and said, "It is not good to take the children's bread and throw it to the little dogs. 27 And she said, "Yes, Lord, yet even the little dogs eat the crumbs which fall from their masters' table." 28 Then Jesus answered and said to her, "O woman, great is your faith! Let it be to you as you desire." And her daughter was healed from that very hour.

D4

Romans 2:1 Therefore you are inexcusable, O man, whoever you are who judge, for in whatever you judge another you condemn yourself; for you who judge practice the same things. 2 But we know that the judgment of God is according to truth against those who practice such things.

D5

1 Thessalonians 1:3 remembering without ceasing your work of faith, labor of love, and patience of hope in our Lord Jesus Christ in the sight of our God and Father, 4 knowing, beloved brethren, your election by God.

D6

Luke 19:10 For the Son of Man has come to seek and to save that which was lost."

WEEK 15

D1

Psalms 119:103 How sweet are Your words to my taste, Sweeterthan honey to my mouth!
104 Through Your precepts I get understanding; Therefore I hate every false way. 105 Your word is a lamp to my feet And a light to my path.

D2

Isaiah 5:24 Therefore, as the fire devours the stubble, And the flame consumes the chaff, So their root will be as rottenness, And their blossom will ascend like dust; Because they have rejected the law of the LORD of hosts, And despised the word of the Holy One of Israel. 25 Therefore the anger of the LORD is aroused against His people; He has stretched out His hand against them And stricken them, And the hills trembled. Their carcasses were as refuse in the midst of the streets. For all this His anger is not turned away, but His hand is stretched out still.

D3

Matthew 12:30 He who is not with Me is against Me, and he who does not gather with Me scatters abroad.

D4

Isaiah 48:16 "Come near to Me, hear this: I have not spoken in secret from the beginning; From the time that it was, I was there. And now the Lord GOD and His Spirit have sent Me." 17 Thus says the LORD, your Redeemer, The Holy One of Israel: "I am the LORD your God, Who teaches you to profit, Who leads you by the way you should go. 18 Oh, that you had heeded My commandments! Then your peace would have been like a river, And your righteousness like the waves of the sea.

D5

John 14:25 "These things I have spoken to you while being present with you. 26 But the Helper, the Holy Spirit, whom the Father will send in My name, He will teach you all things, and bring to your remembrance all things that I said to you. 27 Peace I leave with you, My peace I give to you; not as the world gives do I give to you. Let not your heart be troubled, neither let it be afraid.

D6

1Samuel 15:22 So Samuel said: "Has the LORD as great delight in burnt offerings and sacrifices, As in obeying the voice of the LORD? Behold, to obey is better than sacrifice, And to heed than the fat of rams. 23 For rebellion is as the sin of witchcraft, And stubbornness is as iniquity and idolatry. Because you have rejected the word of the LORD, He also has rejected you from being king."

WEEK 16

D1

Psalms 37:7 Rest in the LORD, and wait patiently for Him; Do not fret because of him who prospers in his way, Because of the man who brings wicked schemes to pass. 8 Cease from anger, and forsake wrath; Do not fret—it only causes harm.

D2

Proverbs 15:13 A merry heart makes a cheerful countenance, But by sorrow of the heart the spirit is broken. 14 The heart of him who has understanding seeks knowledge, But the mouth of fools feeds on foolishness. 15 All the days of the afflicted are evil, But he who is of a merry heart has a continual feast.

D3

Proverbs 14:29 He who is slow to wrath has great understanding, But he who is impulsive exalts folly. 30 A sound heart is life to the body, but envy is rottenness to the bones.

D4

Ecclesiastes 3:12 I know that nothing is better for them than to rejoice, and to do good in their lives, 13 and also that every man should eat and drink and enjoy the good of all his labor—it is the gift of God.

D5

Philippians 2:1 Therefore if there is any consolation in Christ, if any comfort of love, if any fellowship of the Spirit, if any affection and mercy, 2 fulfill my joy by being like-minded, having the same love, being of one accord, of one mind. 3 Let nothing be done through selfish ambition or conceit, but in lowliness of mind let each esteem others better than himself. 4 Let each of you look out not only for his own interests, but also for the interests of others.

D6

1 Timothy 6:6 Now godliness with contentment is great gain. 7 For we brought nothing into this world, and it is certain we can carry nothing out. 8 And having food and clothing, with these we shall be content.

WEEK 17

D1

Philippians 4:4 Rejoice in the Lord always. Again I will say, rejoice! 5 Let your gentleness be known to all men. The Lord is at hand. 6 Be anxious for nothing, but in everything by prayer and supplication, with thanksgiving, let your requests be made known to God; 7 and the peace of God, which surpasses all understanding, will guard your hearts and minds through Christ Jesus.

D2

Micah 6:8 He has shown you, O man, what is good; and what does the LORD require of you but to do justly, to love mercy, and to walk humbly with your God?

D3

1 Thessalonians 5:9 For God did not appoint us to wrath, but to obtain salvation through our Lord Jesus Christ, 10 who died for us, that whether we wake or sleep, we should live together with Him. 11 Therefore comfort each other and edify one another, just as you also are doing.

D4

I Thessalonians 5:17 Pray without ceasing, 18 in everything give thanks; for this is the will of God in Christ Jesus for you.

D5

Jeremiah 31:33 But this is the covenant that I will make with the house of Israel after those days, says the LORD: I will put My law in their minds, and write it on their hearts; and I will be their God, and they shall be My people.34 No more shall every man teach his neighbor, and every man his brother, saying, 'Know the LORD,' for they all shall know Me, from the least of them to the greatest of them, says the LORD. For I will forgive their iniquity, and their sin I will remember no more."

D6

Colossians 2:6 As you therefore have received Christ Jesus the Lord, so walk in Him, 7 rooted and built up in Him and established in the faith, as you have been taught, abounding in it with thanksgiving.

CONTACT INFORMATION FOR:

THE TRANSFORMATION PRINCIPLE

Email:transformationprinciple@gmail.com

Made in United States
North Haven, CT
24 July 2024

55401958R00052